1

JUDITH KNEEN

ENGLISH NOW

Teacher's Book

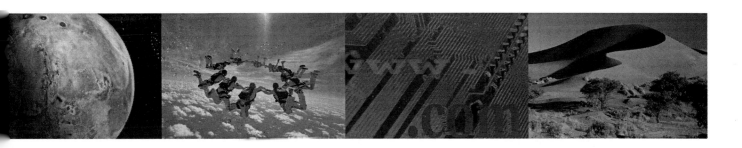

OXFORD
UNIVERSITY PRESS

Contents

Note that the CD accompanying this Teacher's Book contains:
- customizable resources to support the teaching material
  (all of which can be adapted by teachers using PCs)
- assessment material (all of which can be customized by teachers using
  either PCs or Apple Macintosh computers)
- grids showing coverage of Assessment Focuses, Teaching Objectives,
  and cross-curricular links
- interactive activities for individual, paired or group work, all of which
  reinforce literacy skills taught in the Students' Book.

Introduction

English Now is a course for KS3 students working between levels 2+ and 4+. It consists of three students' books, each of which is accompanied by teaching material that includes a CD offering customizable resources and an attractive assortment of interactive student activities to help reinforce basic English skills.

Each book is divided into ten units, which focus on carefully selected topics to ensure a high level of interest for the students. The topics also have strong cross-curricular links, to help raise the standard of English skills used across the whole curriculum, and to reinforce students' understanding that literacy is a life skill and not just relevant to English lessons in school.

How to use *English Now*

Each unit is self-contained, starting with its own contents and introduction, and ending with a 'Challenge' which focuses on specific word and sentence level skills. The intermediate spreads can be used as complete lessons in themselves, each spread being accompanied by a single page of teaching notes which sketches a complete lesson outline (including starter activities, main activities, plenary and extension work).

Assessment for Learning

Assessment for Learning is an integral part of *English Now*. Customizable material is provided on the CD for self-, peer and teacher assessment, and students are encouraged to record their learning objectives at the start of each lesson and to complete the sheet at the end of each lesson. In the Students' Book, there is a prompt at the end of every spread for students to reflect on what skills they have learned, and what areas they may need to revisit.

CD support material

The CD contains customizable resources, including one sheet for each spread of the Students' Book, as well as generic assessment sheets. It also includes grids showing cross-curricular links, the coverage of Assessment Focuses and Teaching Objectives.

CD interactive material

The interactive materials on the CD are designed to engage and motivate the students and to reinforce the English skills taught in the Students' Book. There are four activities linked to each unit, three directly related to practising skills taught in the Students' Book, plus a 'Bonus Game', which is a highly engaging game to reinforce basic spelling. These activities can be played individually, in pairs, or in small groups using a whiteboard.

1 Space

The Solar System

Text type: Information text
Cross-curricular links: Science

Assessment focuses:
Reading
    AF2 Understand, describe, select or retrieve information
Writing
    AF6 Write with technical accuracy of syntax and
    punctuation in phrases, clauses and sentences

Learning objective:
• To develop confidence in reading and writing information
    texts

Learning outcomes:
• To be able to answer questions on a text about space
• To be able to write an information text in proper
    sentences

Framework objectives:
    S13 Conventions of information texts
    R1 Locate information
    R2 Extract information
    Wr11 Present information

Introduction

Ask students to turn to pages 4 and 5 in the Students' Book. Use the Introduction and Shared text to focus them on the unit topic. Ask them to find the spread about 'The Solar System' in the Contents list. Focus on the English skills they will be using. You may wish to give students the self-assessment sheet (**RS A**), to fill in the learning objectives and outcomes.

Starter ideas

a) Engage and stimulate thinking by playing 'Odd-one-out'. Give pairs of students two minutes to discuss which is the odd-one-out: Sun, Mars, Pluto. Discuss their ideas.

b) Simple sentences: For each pair of students, cut up **RS 1.1** into cards. Ask them to use the cards to
    – create a phrase, e.g. nine planets
    – build the phrase into a simple sentence using
        a verb (underlined), e.g. There are <u>nine</u> planets.
    Variations include: lengthening their sentences; reducing the number of cards they use; adding blank cards for their own words.
    Discuss the purpose of these sentences, and where they might find them. Draw attention to the use of present tense.

Lesson development

• **Introduction** Using the text, students should put the five cards with the planets' names (from **RS 1.1**) in their order from the Sun.

• **Facts** Read the text, pointing out that this information text is full of facts – points that can be proved or tested. Give an example.

• Allow students time to respond either verbally or in writing to the questions.

• Q1 – refer students to the glossary.

• Q2 – encourage students to form an opinion.

• Q3 – ask for one fact from everyone to ensure they have grasped the idea.

• **Captions** Each caption makes at least two points, e.g. Venus has 'acid clouds' and 'temperatures up to 480 °C'. Discuss possible captions for Earth. Students can write one on a sticky note. Stick their notes on a globe on the board/flip chart and appraise their ideas.

• **Sentences** Show how to make a caption into a sentence, e.g. Jupiter is a big stormy planet. Challenge them to make two sentences about one planet.

• **Plenary** Shuffle the planet cards (from **RS 1.1**), place them face down and turn them up one at a time. For each planet, students should write down one sentence, giving a fact about the planet.

Extension ideas

• Ask students to list the other features of this information text, e.g. images, heading, sub-headings, present tense. Refer to **RS E** for more features and conventions of information texts.

• Research other information texts on the Solar System, to find examples of these features and conventions.

Teaching support

Support could be directed at:
• preparation of resources, including cards, picture of a globe and sticky notes
• modelling phrases and sentences, using the cards
• helping students to read the captions and questions
• setting up incomplete sentences for students to complete and correct
• working on extension ideas with students.

Assessment

Encourage the students to complete the self-assessment sheet, **RS A**. In addition, **RSs B** and **C** can be used for peer and teacher assessment of learning.

1 Space

Stars, comets, and black holes

Text type: Information
Cross-curricular links: Science

Assessment focuses:
Reading
AF2 Understand, describe, select or retrieve information
Writing
AF7 Select appropriate and effective vocabulary

Learning objectives:
• To write an effective description
• To use words precisely

Learning outcomes:
• To be able to use adjectives to describe stars and comets
• To read, understand, and complete a text on black holes

Framework objectives:
W14 Word meaning in context
R6 Active reading
Wr14 Evocative description
S&L12 Exploratory talk

Introduction

Ask students to turn to pages 4 and 5 in the Students' Book. Use the Introduction and Shared text to focus them on the unit topic. Ask them to find the spread about 'Stars, comets, and black holes' in the Contents list. Focus on the English skills they will be using. You may wish to give students the self-assessment sheet (**RS A**), to fill in the learning objectives and outcomes.

Starter ideas

a) Play the adjectives game. Choose a theme, e.g. animals. Starting with 'a', go around the class and ask each student to name an animal and an adjective, starting with each letter of the alphabet, e.g. awful antelope, bubbly baboon.

b) Give students a few sentences which have overused adjectives, such as 'nice' or 'good', e.g. Her new mobile was really good. Ask them to think of alternatives, e.g. smart, neat.

Lesson development

• **Introduction** Read the information on galaxies, comets, and supernovae and check students' understanding.
• **Adjectives** Read out the words given in Q1. Ensure students can say the words, understand their meaning and how adjectives are used. Use **RS 1.2** to emphasize how adjectives give us a clearer picture of something by highlighting different qualities. Discuss their ideas. The most suitable ones are: size – giant, vast; brightness –

glowing, blazing; shape – swirling, spiralling; strength – powerful, violent.
• **Selecting adjectives** Ask pairs to discuss which adjectives would best describe a galaxy, comet and supernova. Encourage them to consider both text and pictures.
• **Adjectives in writing** Ask individuals to write a proper sentence about each picture, accurately using the adjectives they have been considering, e.g. A blazing comet zoomed across the sky.
• **Black holes** Complete the activity on black holes, again encouraging precision.
• **Plenary** Read successful examples of the students' sentences using adjectives. They should rate the sentence out of five, either with a show of fingers or a numbered slip of paper.
• Alternatively, give a student an adjective (possibly one used in the lesson). He or she must describe it, without using the word, for the rest of the class to guess it.

Extension ideas

• Challenge students to use a thesaurus to find synonyms of an adjective they have used, e.g. bright. Ensure they choose only adjectives.
• Ask students to find out more about galaxies, comets and supernovae. They could design a short cloze exercise (like the black holes one) for a partner to complete.

Teaching support

The main part of the lesson could be organized as a guided writing session. Learning support staff can:
• lead a guided group
• review student understanding of the task
• check student strategies
• support their attempts
• help students to evaluate their writing.

Support could also be directed at:
• preparation of resources
• working on extension ideas with students
• collecting examples of good work to share in the plenary.

Assessment

Encourage the students to complete the self-assessment sheet, **RS A**. In addition, **RSs B** and **C** can be used for peer and teacher assessment of learning.

1 Space

Is anybody out there?

Text type: Information, Poetry
Cross-curricular links: Science

Assessment focuses:
Reading
   AF3 Deduce, infer or interpret information, events or
   ideas from texts
Writing
   AF1 Write imaginative and interesting texts

Learning objectives:
• To encourage the use of talk to clarify and explain
• To develop inference and deduction skills

Learning outcomes:
• To design and explain a space time capsule
• To work out poetry riddle and write their own

Framework objectives:
   R8 Infer and deduce
   Wr9 Link writing and reading
   S&L1 Clarify through talk
   S&L4 Answers, instructions, explanations

Introduction

Ask students to turn to pages 4 and 5 in the
Students' Book. Use the Introduction and Shared
text to focus them on the unit topic. Ask them to
find the spread entitled 'Is anybody out there?' in the
Contents list. Focus on the English skills they will be
using. You may wish to give students the self-
assessment sheet (**PCM A**), to fill in the learning
objectives and outcomes.

Starter idea

Play 'Twenty questions'. Students have 20 questions
to guess an item you have chosen. Reveal whether it
is animal (an animal, person or derived from animal),
mineral (inorganic item, such as metal) or vegetable
(plants or derived from plants). You may only answer
yes or *no*.

The game develops questioning for clarification.
Review their performance, e.g. Were their initial
questions broad enough? Did they listen to all the
answers? Did they make deductions?

Lesson development

• **Introduction** Read through the information
  text on page 10. Explain the idea of a disk or
  time capsule being sent out into space with
  information about Earth.

• **Aliens** Ask students to consider potential
  communication problems, e.g. different beings,
  technologies, communications. Then discuss what
  we could tell aliens about Earth.

• **Disk** Allow students to work in pairs to help
  stimulate ideas.

• Q1 – challenge them to make their own
  message exactly 10 words long. This will help
  focus the task. Encourage a range of sounds,
  e.g. music, voices, water, and pictures,
  e.g. animals, plants, maps.

• Q2 – a framework may help to encourage
  explanations, e.g. I have chosen… *[the sound of
  the sea]* because… *[sea covers so much of the Earth]*.

• **An alien visit to Earth** On page 11 students
  are asked to imagine an alien visiting Earth.
  Discuss what it might find puzzling, e.g. trees,
  clothes, television.

• **A riddle** In pairs, encourage the students to
  work out what is referred to by the extracts from
  Craig Raine's poem 'A Martian Sends a Postcard
  Home'. Extract A is a car, extract B is time, and
  extract C is dreams.

• **Writing a riddle** Students should attempt to
  write their own riddle in the same style. Possible
  ideas might be: *comb, kettle, balloon*.

• **Plenary** Read out examples of students' riddles,
  and encourage the rest of the group to guess
  the answers.

Extension ideas

• Give students **PCM 1.3** to see further extracts of
  the poem 'A Martian Sends a Postcard Home'.
  Note that Caxtons are books, and 'a haunted
  apparatus' is a baby.

Teaching support

Support might include:
• prompting students' questions in the starter activity
• encouraging students to explain their choices for
  the space time capsule, through the use of words
  such as: *because… which will… so that…*
• helping students to generate a range of ideas for
  the space disk
• modelling the writing of basic riddles
• working on extension ideas.

Assessment

Encourage the students to complete the self-
assessment sheet, **RS A**. In addition, **RSs B**
and **C** can be used for peer and teacher assessment
of learning.

1 Space

People in space

Text type: Information
Cross-curricular links: Science

Assessment focuses:
Reading
   AF2 Understand, describe, select or retrieve information, events or ideas from texts and use quotation and reference to text
Writing
   AF3 Organize and present texts, sequencing and structuring information, ideas and events

Learning objectives:
• To be able to access information from texts using both text and graphics
• To be able to produce information texts, using existing texts and from their own ideas

Learning outcomes:
• To produce an entry for an encyclopedia
• To design, describe and explain a new space suit

Framework objectives:
R1 Locate information
R2 Extract information
Wr10 Organize texts appropriately
Wr11 Present information

Introduction

Ask students to turn to pages 4 and 5 in the Students' Book. Use the Introduction and Shared text to focus them on the unit topic. Ask them to find the spread about 'People in space', in the Contents list. Focus on the English skills they will be using. You may wish to give students the self-assessment sheet (**PCM A**), to fill in the learning objectives and outcomes.

Starter idea

Write the following words large on separate pieces of paper: *text, photo, graph, diagram, table, picture, caption, heading,* and *label*. Give each 'poster' to a student and ask them to hold them up at the front of the class. Next, read out some types of information text, e.g. dictionary, encyclopedia, newspaper, text book. If they are holding a possible 'ingredient' of that text, they should stand forward. The individual or the whole class can decide.

Lesson development

• **Introduction** Read through the text on page 12. Give students time to match the parts of a space shuttle in the text and in the picture.
   The orbiter = the main craft
   Three main engines = circular parts at the rear of the orbiter.

Two rocket boosters = two large white cylinders
Fuel tank = the large rust-coloured cylinder

• **Encyclopedias** Use **PCM 1.4** to show the possible features of an encyclopedia entry. This indicates presentational features and how information texts can be made up of description, explanation, facts and figures. Additional features could be bullet points, diagrams, graphs, maps, captions.

• **Writing an entry** Introduce the writing task. Encourage students to utilize the information (as opposed to copying it) by giving them focus areas, such as why the Shuttle is unique, describing what it looks like; historic space flights. Alternatively, give topic sentence starters: e.g. The Space Shuttle is special because…

• **Space suits** Read the information on living in space and ask students to design their own suit. Draw attention to the fact that although they will be producing an information text, it includes explanation and description. Information texts are often hybrid texts.

• **Plenary** Using the spread as the source, students should write one quiz question on people in space. Collect the questions in and, with some careful selection, hold a quiz. Allow them to use the book to check their answers.

Extension ideas

• Look for examples of other graphic information texts on people in space and compare the presentation with the pictures in the Students' Book. What alternative information do they give? (The NASA website is excellent – www.nasa.gov/missions/highlights/index.html)

Teaching support

Support could be directed at:
• preparing posters for the starters
• modelling how to search the texts for information
• supporting the planning of writing, e.g. referring students back to the models available in the text, providing sentence starters, suggesting a simple structure.

Assessment

Encourage the students to complete the self-assessment sheet, **RS A**. In addition, **RSs B** and **C** can be used for peer and teacher assessment of learning.

1 Space

Disaster

Text type: Playscript
Cross-curricular links: Science

Assessment focuses:
Writing
 AF1 Write imaginative and interesting texts
 AF2 Produce texts which are appropriate to task, reader and purpose

Learning objectives:
• To develop understanding of the layout and purpose of scripts
• To know how to write a script

Learning outcomes:
• To explore an extract from a script about *Apollo 13*
• To plan and write a short script

Framework objectives:
 Wr1 Drafting process
 Wr9 Link writing and reading
 S&L16 Collaborate on scripts
 S&L17 Extend spoken repertoire

Introduction

Ask students to turn to pages 4 and 5 in the Students' Book. Use the Introduction and Shared text to focus them on the unit topic. Ask them to find the spread about 'Disasters' in the Contents list. Focus on the English skills they will be using. You may wish to give students the self-assessment sheet (**PCM A**), to fill in the learning objectives and outcomes.

Starter ideas

a) Assess prior knowledge by asking students to list three facts about scripts, e.g. characters names go on the left, actors use them. Discuss their ideas.

b) Introduce relevant vocabulary by putting the following words on the board with one or two letters missing from each: *character, script, play, film, directions, props, stage, set*. Ask students what the words are and what they mean.

Lesson development

• **Introduction** Read through the introductory text and the script on page 14. Discuss the talking points and encourage students to explore saying the final line in different ways.
• **Directions** Ask students to think of a suitable word to insert in a 'directions' bracket, if it were included on the final line, i.e. (…) *Houston, we have a problem.*

• **Action reading** In threes, students can prepare an action reading of the extract, acting it out with the help of their books. They will not need a lot of space – spacecraft are compact! View and comment on their interpretation of the script.
• **Script layout** Review the conventions for script writing. You might draw attention to: characters' names are often written in a 'margin'; use of the colon; lack of speech marks; bracketing of directions; some short lines/incomplete sentences.
• **Writing a script** Read the information and the task on page 15. Students are to write the next part of the script. **PCM 1.5** will help students to plan what the characters say. You may wish to give them time to discuss their ideas in pairs.
• **Disasters** Discuss what they know of other space disasters and read the remaining text of the page. Allow plenty of time to discuss Q5.
• **Plenary idea** Play 'Taboo' with vocabulary used in the starter activity. Students must explain what a word means, e.g. character, without saying the word itself. You could also introduce taboo words that must not be used, e.g. lines, actor.

Extension ideas

• View the film *Apollo 13* (1995, PG) so that students can compare their version with the film version.
• Allow students to give an action reading of the scripts that they have written.

Teaching support

If the writing is undertaken during a guided writing session, support staff can lead a guided group by
• revising the conventions of a script
• supporting planning
• giving time for independent writing
• regularly reviewing writing.

Support could also be with
• preparation of resources
• prompting students on the starter and plenary tasks.

Assessment

Encourage the students to complete the self-assessment sheet, **RS A**. In addition, **RSs B** and **C** can be used for peer and teacher assessment of learning.

1 Space

Space challenge

Introduction

This final section is designed to test word and sentence level skills. It gives students the opportunity to complete short tasks independently.

The skills are linked to other parts of the unit but the activities stand alone. Students do not need to look back at the rest of the unit, although you may wish to draw their attention to the links as you review their work.

There are two suggested approaches:
1. Students start at number 1 and are allowed to work their way though the activities at their own pace. There are extension ideas for some of the activities for those students who may require them.
2. Allow students time to complete one activity and review it together before moving on to the next task. This may be more supportive to those students who have difficulty working independently.

Task 1

Focus: alphabetical order

The correct order is:
Earth   Jupiter   Mars   Mercury   Saturn   Venus

Extension: Apart from Mars and Mercury, the alphabetical order is dependent on the first letter. Provide a list which requires them to focus further on second letters, e.g.
- Mars   Moon   Mercury
- star   Sun   solar   Saturn.

Task 2

Focus: adjectives and nouns

a. Possible products are:
Galaxy (chocolate bar and vehicle)
Mars (chocolate bar and company)
Milky Way (chocolate bar)
Comet (store)
The Sun (newspaper)
The Mercury (newspaper)
The Star (newspaper)

b. If students have difficulty thinking up adjectives and nouns, ask them to underline the adjectives and/or nouns in these sentences:
- *The Sun* is a daily paper.
- Galaxy is creamy chocolate.
- Comet is a huge store.

Task 3

Focus: the prefix 'super'.

The answers are:
a. supermarket
b. superpower
c. superheroes.

Other words using this prefix include:
superglue
superhuman
superman
supernatural
superstore
supertanker.

Task 4

Focus: punctuation of a script

The text should be punctuated as follows:

SAM: Quick! We don't have much time.
ANDY: What can I do?
SAM: Shut down the engine.
ANDY: When?
SAM: (shouting) Now!

Extension: Ask students to continue the script, ensuring they use the correct punctuation.

Assessment

RS D can be used for self- and teacher assessment of the work done on the unit challenge spreads.

Extended text

There is an extended text, linked to the unit topic on **RS 1.6**. This can be used in a variety of ways to extend the students' skills and to engage them further.

2 Natural disasters

Earth

Introduction

Ask students to turn to pages 18 and 19 in the Students' Book. Use the Introduction and Shared text to focus them on the unit topic. Ask them to find the spread about 'Earth' in the Contents list. Focus on the English skills they will be using. You may wish to give students the self-assessment sheet (**RS A**), to fill in the learning objectives and outcomes.

Starter idea

'Maps from memory' is a great game for focusing on reading a map.
• Use a simple map (e.g. UK outline, local area, school) that only you have.
• Put students into groups of four. In each group, number students 1 to 4.
• Explain it is a competition to draw the best map.
• Call up all the number 1s. Give them 45 seconds to study your map, then 45 seconds to return to their groups and draw what they have seen, watched carefully by the others.
• Repeat with the 2s, 3s and 4s.
• Judge the best map, and discuss the reading skills they used.

Lesson development

• **Introduction** Introduce the map of the world. Draw attention to the features of the map including the key. Check the students understand what they are seeing before you move on to the activities.
• Q1 - Encourage pairs to make notes on what the map reveals about earthquakes. Prompt them if necessary:
    – *In what parts of the world do they occur?*
    – *Is there a pattern?*
    – *Are earthquakes likely in the UK?*
• Q2 - Join pairs into fours to share their ideas, then discuss their findings as a class.
• Q3 - Ask individuals to write a fact about earthquakes. (Draw attention to the Help box.) You may wish to give a sentence starter, e.g. The map shows that…
• **Reading** Read the information about earthquakes. The emphasis and pauses in your voice can give the students clues as to the structure of the text. Check their understanding.
• Q4 - The task is to paragraph the text. Draw attention to the Help box which will guide them. Remind them that an indentation shows the beginning of a paragraph. Use **RS 2.1** to compare the text with and without paragraphs. Discuss how:
    – they help the reader by dividing up the text
    – changes in subject or angle may cue a new paragraph
    – the initial 'topic' sentence is often supported by the rest, e.g. expansion, explanation, exemplification.
• **Plenary** Ask students to discuss what they have learned, and to report back (in one sentence) on what their partner has learned.

Extension idea

Study another information text to see how the text is divided into paragraphs. Discuss why and when to start a new paragraph, e.g. to change the topic, time, idea.

Teaching support

Support could be directed at:
• being the 'map holder' in the starter activity
• prompting students on notes, sentences and paragraphs.

Assessment

Encourage the students to complete the self-assessment sheet, **RS A**. In addition, **RSs B** and **C** can be used for peer and teacher assessment of learning.

2 Natural disasters

Fire

Text type: Information, Recount
Cross-curricular links: Geography

Assessment focuses:
Reading
   AF5 Explain and comment on writers' use of language
Writing
   AF6 Write with technical accuracy of syntax and punctuation
   AF7 Select appropriate and effective vocabulary

Learning objectives:
• To recognize that complex sentences are made up of clauses
• To be able to comment on the use of imagery

Learning outcomes:
• To build complex sentences about volcanoes
• To explain the effect of some images written about a volcano

Framework objectives:
   S1 Subordinate clauses
   R13 Non-fiction style
   R14 Language choices
   Wr8 Visual and sound effects

Introduction

Ask students to turn to pages 18 and 19 in the Students' Book. Use the Introduction and Shared text to focus them on the unit topic. Ask them to find the spread about 'Fire' in the Contents list. Focus on the English skills they will be using. You may wish to give students the self-assessment sheet (**RS A**), to fill in the learning objectives and outcomes.

Starter idea

Play 'Sentence odd-one-out'. Write three sentences on the board: two simple and one complex, e.g.
• Mount Etna is in Italy.
• It is a volcano.
• When it erupted in 1669, it killed about 100,000 people.
Give pairs one minute to discuss the differences, and then take feedback. Draw out that the third example is a complex sentence, made up of two clauses, divided by a comma.

Lesson development

• **Introduction** Give the students time to study the diagram of the erupting volcano and draw attention to the labels.

• Q1 – Students should use the diagram labels to complete the complex sentences. Use **RS 2.2** to analyse the complex sentences, e.g. highlight the main/subordinate clauses and their relative positions. Experiment with writing the clauses in a different order.
• Q2 – Encourage the students to match the adjectives with the picture of the erupting volcano. Ask them to explain their choices.
• **Reading** The description of Vesuvius erupting is from the account of an early volcanologist, William Hamilton. Written in an age before photography, Hamilton's words are particularly vivid and descriptive. Discuss which words are most effective.
• Q3 – Ask the students to complete the comments on the language and imagery. Encourage thoughtful responses that focus on the images, e.g. *This suggests that the mountain is alive.* Or *This suggests that the mountain is spewing out fire.*
• Q4 – Draw attention to the use of metaphors in the description, using the Help box. Encourage students to create their own metaphor for lava, e.g. *a river of lava, a fiery wave, a crawling monster.*
• **Plenary** Play the 'Metaphor game'. Brainstorm the qualities and uses of fire, then give pairs of students one minute to think up a metaphor for *fire*. Note down their ideas and use them as the basis for an effective class poem.

Extension ideas

• Ask students to write their own complex sentences about volcanoes.
• Consider the functions of complex sentences, e.g. how they can give further information, develop ideas and elaborate descriptions.

Teaching support

Support could be directed at:
• monitoring students' progress and prompting them where necessary, e.g. with the examples given in the Lesson development, above
• scribing the responses to the 'Metaphor game' in the plenary, and building them into a class metaphor poem for display.

Assessment

Encourage the students to complete the self-assessment sheet, **RS A**. In addition, **RSs B** and **C** can be used for peer and teacher assessment of learning.

2 Natural disasters

Water

Text type: Reports
Cross-curricular links: Geography

Assessment focuses:
Reading
  AF2 Understand, describe, select or retrieve information, events or ideas from texts
  AF3 Deduce, infer or interpret information, events or ideas from texts
Writing
  AF2 Write texts which are appropriate to tasks, reader and purpose

Learning objectives:
* To be able to extract information, as well as infer and deduce information, from headlines and pictures
* To understand how headlines work

Learning outcomes:
* To analyse some headlines about a tsunami
* To write a headline to go with a photograph

Framework objectives:
  R2 Extract information
  R8 Infer and deduce
  Wr11 Present information
  S&L1 Clarify through talk

Introduction

Ask students to turn to pages 18 and 19 in the Students' Book. Use the Introduction and Shared text to focus them on the unit topic. Ask them to find the spread about 'Water' in the Contents list. Focus on the English skills they will be using. You may wish to give students the self-assessment sheet (**RS A**), to fill in the learning objectives and outcomes.

Starter idea

Play 'Clues'. The aim is to extract as much information as possible from clues. Put students into small groups and give each group a slip of paper. Explain that you are going to give them three clues to help guess a subject. If they guess after the first clue, they gain 5 points, after the second 3 points, and after the last clue 1 point. They only have one guess and can submit it when they want. Try to make the clues increasingly easy, e.g.
Subject: Asian tsunami
Clue 1: hundreds of thousands died
Clue 2: bad floods
Clue 3: 26 December 2004

Lesson development

* **Introduction** Draw attention to the two diagrams on page 24. Model how to read the main features, e.g. the images and the labels.
* Q1 - Direct students to the Help box, and encourage them to ask questions that start in different ways, e.g. Where do tsunami start? What causes tsunami?
* Q2 - Encourage them to refer to the text for answers, rather than guessing.
* Q3 - The Help box gives suggestions for how to improve questioning.
* Read the headlines about the Asian tsunami. Explain that headlines provide clues as to what the reports are about. Discuss what they think the reports will be about, as well as what they know about the tragedy.
* Q4 - **RS 2.3** may be used here, giving students space to annotate the headlines, jot down ideas and make notes.
* Q5 - Encourage students to think carefully about the techniques used in the headlines, e.g. Drama - '*a deadly wall*', Emotion - '*which child to save*'.
* Q6 - Refer the students to the Help box and encourage them to use at least one of the techniques.
* **Plenary** Ask students to write a headline, using no more than eight words, about the lesson. For example, '*Students hit by headlines in tsunami lesson*', '*"Reading helped me understand tsunami" reveals student*', '*Students' questions amaze teacher!*'

Extension ideas

* Write the first sentence or paragraph of a report that could go under one of these headlines.
* Investigate some of the newspaper reports themselves, looking, for example at the *Guardian* newspaper archive www.guardian.co.uk.

Teaching support

Support could involve:
* preparing clues before the starter game
* modelling how to explore and annotate the headlines
* prompting students to write their own headlines.

Assessment

Encourage the students to complete the self-assessment sheet, **RS A**. In addition, **RSs B** and **C** can be used for peer and teacher assessment.

2 Natural disasters

Wind

Text type: Poetry, Recount
Cross-curricular links: Geography

Assessment focuses:
Reading
  AF5 Explain and comment on writers' use of language
Writing
  AF1 Write imaginative, interesting and thoughtful texts
  AF7 Select appropriate and effective vocabulary

Learning objectives:
• To understand and use some poetic techniques

Learning outcomes:
• To recognize the use of personification in a poem about the wind
• To write a poem about a tornado, using personification

Framework objectives:
  R12 Character, setting and mood
  Wr8 Visual and sound effects
  Wr9 Link writing and reading

Introduction

Ask students to turn to pages 18 and 19 in the Students' Book. Use the Introduction and Shared text to focus them on the unit topic. Ask them to find the spread about 'Wind' in the Contents list. Focus on the English skills they will be using. You may wish to give students the self-assessment sheet (**RS A**), to fill in the learning objectives and outcomes.

Starter idea

Give pairs two minutes to discuss the typical features of a poem and then complete a sentence which starts: *In a poem, you might find…* If necessary, prompt with ideas such as: rhyme, rhythm, alliteration, similes, etc.

Lesson development

• **Introduction** Read the poem 'I am the Wind' and ensure understanding of content and vocabulary.
• Q1   Explore how the writer uses verbs to bring actions and movement to the poem. Students should list how the wind moves in the poem by identifying the verbs. Use **RS 2.4** which provides a copy of the poem for students to annotate. Draw attention to how the present participles, e.g. running, blowing, give the impression of ongoing, non-stop action.
• Q2 – Use the Help box to explain personification. Again, students may use **RS 2.4** to highlight personification, e.g. 'I fight the trees', 'Stealing hats'.
• Q3 – Discuss the character of the wind. Encourage students to refer to the poem for evidence, e.g. I think the wind is daring and rude because it blows clouds across the sun's face.

• **Tornadoes** Read the newspaper extract about tornadoes and encourage students to share their knowledge of twisters.
• Q4 – Encourage students to write a poem about tornadoes, following the format of the poem 'I am the Wind'. You may wish to teach this as a guided writing session (see below). Use the Help box to support their planning. Encourage plenty of action and the use of personification. For their final presentation, they may wish to create a shape poem – in a twisting shape – or a mobile of (literally) moving words.
• **Plenary** Share and enjoy examples of the students' writing. Appraise the techniques used.

Extension idea

Explore other examples of poems which use personification, e.g. 'March' by Emily Dickinson (**RS 2.6**) or 'The Tide in the River' by Eleanor Farjeon.

Guided writing

This sequence may be helpful:
• Review the task
• Review the features of the poem 'I am the Wind'
• Create a bank of words and descriptions (see Help box)
• Model and practise using personification
• Draft initial ideas with support
• Consider structure and presentation
• Promote independent redrafting
• Review and evaluate.
See **RSs G** and **H** for notes and planning for guided work.

Teaching support

Support could be directed at:
• leading a guided group
• looking for work to be read out at the end
• supporting extension work.

Assessment

Encourage the students to complete the self-assessment sheet, **RS A**. In addition, **RSs B** and **C** can be used for peer and teacher assessment.

2 Natural disasters

Surviving a flood

Text type: Advice
Cross-curricular links: Geography

Assessment focuses:
Writing
    AF2 Produce texts which are appropriate to task, reader and purpose
    AF3 Organize and present whole texts effectively, sequencing and structuring information, ideas and events

Learning objectives:
• To understand the conventions of writing to advise

Learning outcomes:
• To collaborate on the planning and drafting of an advice leaflet about flooding

Framework objectives:
    Wr13 Instructions and directions
    Wr17 Informal advice
    S&L13 Collaboration
    S&L15 Explore in role

Introduction

Ask students to turn to pages 18 and 19 in the Students' Book. Use the Introduction and Shared text to focus them on the unit topic. Ask them to find the spread about 'Surviving a flood' in the Contents list. Focus on the English skills they will be using. You may wish to give students the self-assessment sheet (**RS A**), to fill in the learning objectives and outcomes.

Starter idea

Words of advice: ask students to think of five words or phrases that may be helpful when giving advice. Encourage them to think of imperatives such as 'try', 'don't', 'make sure'.

Lesson development

• **Introduction** Read the main text on floods and consider how floods are one form of natural disaster that is a real danger in many parts of the UK. Millions of people risk flooding every year.
• Q1 – Put students into small groups and before they write anything, encourage them to talk about the problems caused by floods, e.g. loss of electricity, lack of clean water, risk of infections. Suggest that they prioritize issues.
• Q2 and 3 – Read the tips and let them feed into the students' own ideas. Encourage students to make notes under three headings: what to do 1) before a flood, 2) during a flood, 3) after a flood.

• Q4 – Create an advice leaflet on surviving a flood. This part of the lesson could be organized as a guided writing session (see below). **RS 2.5** provides a framework for students to follow. Encourage students to:
    – use the three-fold structure
    – refer to the Help box
    – consider presentational issues, e.g. headings, sub-heading and bullets.
• **Plenary** Compose a sentence, giving advice to a younger student on one key aspect of writing advice.

Extension ideas

• Compare the students' leaflets with official advice. For example, the BBC weather website has a clear page of advice at www.bbc.co.uk/weather/features/flood_action.shtml.
• Investigate the effects of actual floods in the UK, e.g. the famous floods of 1953 (www.bbc.co.uk/weather/features/understanding/1953_flood.shtml), or more recently those at Boscastle in August 2004.

Guided writing

This sequence may be helpful:
• Review the task
• Review the features of the advice texts (see help box)
• Model and practise using certain techniques, e.g. giving instructions and using reassurance
• Draft initial ideas with support
• Consider structure and presentation
• Promote independent redrafting
• Review and evaluate.
See **RSs G** and **H** for notes and planning for guided work.

Teaching support

Support could be directed at:
• leading a guided group
• modelling and prompting how to give advice
• supporting extension work.

Assessment

Encourage the students to complete the self-assessment sheet, **RS A**. In addition, **RSs B** and **C** can be used for peer and teacher assessment.

Natural disasters challenge

Introduction

This final section is designed to test word and
sentence level skills. It gives students the opportunity
to complete short tasks independently.

The skills are linked to other parts of the unit but
the activities stand alone. Students do not need to
look back at the rest of the unit, although you may
wish to draw their attention to the links as you
review their work.

There are two suggested approaches:
1. Students start at number 1 and work their way
    though the activities at their own pace. There are
    extension ideas for some of the activities for
    those students who may require them.
2. Allow students time to complete one activity and
    review it together before moving on to the next
    task. This may be more supportive to those students
    who have difficulty working independently.

Task 1

Focus: alphabetical order

The correct order is:
Alberto
Chris
Debby
Nadine
Patty
Tony.

Extension:

*   Students can create their own list of names for
    hurricanes. They must alternate between boys'
    and girls' names, and the names must be in
    alphabetical order.
*   If students want to investigate hurricane names
    further, the full lists of names can be found at
    www.fema.gov/kids/hunamcs3.htm.

Task 2

Focus: plurals

The answers are:
*   volcanoes
*   potatoes
*   tomatoes
*   tornadoes
*   heroes
*   echoes.

Extension: Most nouns ending in 'o' just need an 's'
to make the plural. Ask students to add an 's' to these
words to make the plurals: solo, piano, zoo, disco, radio.

Task 3

Focus: personification

Here are the examples of personification from the
text, with possible explanations of the effect of the
words. Compare these ideas with those given by the
students.
*   'water creeps' – *suggests the water is being cautious
    and secretive*
*   'It hates land' – *it possesses strong feelings*
*   'It wants to smother' – *it is aggressive and dangerous
    – it can kill*
*   'it can see' – *gives the impression that the water is
    watchful*
*   'the ruler' – *this tells us that water is in control*
*   'just weaklings' – *they are weak and powerless*
*   'water will win' – *water is engaged in a battle or
    competition.*

Task 4

Focus: using words with precision

Ensure that students have understood the specific
meanings of the words, and that their responses are
not too general. Here are examples of how the
words might be used:
*   A gentle <u>breeze</u> rustled the leaves.
*   The <u>gale</u> stripped the leaves from the trees.
*   Buildings and cars were sucked up by the <u>tornado</u>.
*   The <u>hurricane</u> brought strong winds and floods
    to the coast of Texas.
*   The boat was tossed about by the sudden <u>squall</u>.
*   One strong <u>gust</u> tipped the boat over.

Assessment

RS D can be used for self- and teacher assessment
of the work done on the unit challenge spreads.

Extended text

There is an extended text, linked to the unit topic, on
RS 2.6. This can be used in a variety of ways to
extend the students' skills and to engage them further.

The world wide web

Text type: Web pages
Cross-curricular links: ICT

Assessment focuses:
Reading
    AF4 Identify and comment on the structure and
    organization of texts
Writing
    AF3 Organize and present whole texts effectively

Learning objectives:
• To recognize good and bad features of a web page layout

Learning outcomes:
• To label the features of a web page
• To spot bad design features and redesign a web page

Framework objectives:
    R10 Media audiences
    R11 Print, sound and image
    Wr10 Organize texts appropriately

Introduction

Ask students to turn to pages 32 and 33 in the Students' Book. Use the Introduction and Shared text to focus them on the unit topic. Ask them to find the spread about 'The world wide web' in the Contents list. Focus on the English skills they will be using. You may wish to give students the self-assessment sheet (**RS A**), to fill in the learning objectives and outcomes.

Starter ideas

• Play '60-second challenge', giving pairs one minute to write down all the presentational and/or structural features of a web page, e.g. headings, pictures.
• Play 'Know, don't know', by giving the students a list of relevant terms (e.g. text, images, links, navigation bar) and asking them to sort them into the words they know, and those they don't. Discuss and explain the terms.

Lesson development

• **Introduction** Read through the introductory text and look at The Wildlife Trust web page.
• **Labelling** Ask students to consider the labels and what they refer to on the web page. They should write two more labels. Refer them to the Help box, and encourage explanations of the features.
• **Bad design** These next two sections of the lesson might be whole class or organized as a guided reading session (see below). Read the introductory text and draw attention to the badly designed web page for a sports centre.

Allow time to discuss the poor features. Refer to the panel which lists bad design features, for ideas.
• **Good design** Explore how the design might be improved. Ask students to list the changes they would make. Use the framework provided by **RS 3.1** or the headings in the Help box to structure their ideas. Finally, they can sketch out and label a diagram of an improved web page.
• **Plenary** Give students one of these sentences to finish:
Good web page design means…
Bad web page design means…
Review their ideas.

Extension ideas

• Develop their sketches of an improved web page into a proper computer presented version.
• Find and analyse other examples of poorly designed web pages.

Guided reading

This sequence may be helpful:
• Remind students of the objective – to look for bad design
• Review what they are looking for, using the box giving bad design features
• Allow pairs time to read and discuss the text.
• As a group, discuss their ideas for improvements
• Working individually, they should create a list of improvements. Support those who need it.
• Share their ideas, and review what they have learned.
See **RSs G** and **H** for notes and planning for guided work.

Teaching support

Support could be directed at:
• supporting a guided group
• preparation of resources
• prompting students on the starter and plenary tasks.

Assessment

Encourage the students to complete the self-assessment sheet, **RS A**. In addition, **RSs B** and **C** can be used for peer and teacher assessment.

3 The Internet

The net

Text type: Information, Explanation
Cross-curricular links: ICT

Assessment focuses:
Reading
- AF2 Understand, describe, select or retrieve information, events or ideas from texts

Learning objectives:
- To understand and use some of the specialist ICT words and terms

Learning outcomes:
- To understand the meaning of some common abbreviations used in ICT
- To follow an explanation, involving specialist ICT vocabulary

Framework objectives:
W21 Subject vocabulary
R1 Locate information
R2 Extract information

Introduction

Ask students to turn to pages 32 and 33 in the Students' Book. Use the Introduction and Shared text to focus them on the unit topic. Ask them to find the spread about 'The net' in the Contents list. Focus on the English skills they will be using. You may wish to give students the self-assessment sheet (**RS A**), to fill in the learning objectives and outcomes.

Starter idea

Play 'Abbreviation pairs', which is a good game for kinaesthetic learners. Create domino cards with an abbreviation on one side and the full version on the other. Cut them in half, mix them up and give one 'half' to each student. They must each find their other half. Examples of abbreviations: e.g./for example; FC/football club; utd/united; PM/prime minister; CD/compact disk; TV/television; BBC/British Broadcasting Corporation; exam/examination.

Lesson development

- **Introduction** Read through the introductory text about the Internet and why we use it. Other reasons for using the Internet might include: shopping, selling things, sending electronic cards, etc. Other possible questions are: *How do you use the Internet? Is the Internet easy to use? Could we do without the Internet?*

- **Abbreviations** Ensure students understand what an abbreviation is (refer to the glossary and the starter). Introduce the activity on matching abbreviations and meanings. Ask them to copy the table and fill in the answers, or hand out copies of **RS 3.2** for recording their responses. Direct them to the Help box for the answers. The answers are:
  - www = world wide web
  - e-mail = electronic mail
  - .sch = school
  - ISP = internet service provider
  - FAQ = frequently asked questions.
  Check understanding, and whether they know any more abbreviations related to the Internet or computers.

- **Internet maze** Challenge students to complete this reading task. They must follow the six steps to find their way through the maze. A variation on this is to ask one student to read the explanation to another student, who listens and follows the steps. Once they have completed the route from your computer to the USA, they can list the steps back again. This might be a verbal or a written list.

- **Plenary** Give pairs of students one minute to think of an answer to either/both of these questions:
  - *Why are so many abbreviations used in ICT?*
  - *Why are abbreviations useful?*

Extension ideas

- Find other examples of computer abbreviations, e.g. RAM or MB, and find out what they mean.
- Ask students to create their own maze/ explanation for a similar process, such as sending an e-mail.

Teaching support

Support could be directed at:
- preparing resources, e.g. domino cards
- prompting and questioning students on the tasks and discussions
- monitoring students' progress through the activities and promoting extension tasks where appropriate.

Assessment

Encourage the students to complete the self-assessment sheet, **RS A**. In addition, **RSs B** and **C** can be used for peer and teacher assessment.

3 The Internet

Talking on the net

Text type: Persusasive, Instructions
Cross-curricular links: ICT

Assessment focuses:
Reading
   AF3 Deduce, infer or interpret information, events or
   ideas from texts
   AF6 Identify and comment on writers' purposes and
   viewpoints and the overall effect of the text on the reader

Learning objectives:
• To understand some of the purposes and problems of
   communicating on the Internet

Learning outcomes:
• To recognize some of the good and bad points of e-mail
• To decide on safe and polite behaviour on the Internet

Framework objectives:
   R7 Identify main ideas
   R8 Infer and deduce
   S&L1 Clarify through talk
   S&L10 Report main points

Introduction

Ask students to turn to pages 32 and 33 in the Students' Book. Use the Introduction and Shared text to focus them on the unit topic. Ask them to find the spread about 'Talking on the net' in the Contents list. Focus on the English skills they will be using. You may wish to give students the self-assessment sheet (**RS A**), to fill in the learning objectives and outcomes.

Starter idea

E-mail or snail mail? Ask students to consider which they would use for the following and why:

a) Arranging an evening out with a friend (*E-mail, because it's quick and informal.*)

b) A letter to the headteacher to apologize for a broken window (*A proper letter is more formal.*)

c) A letter to a penfriend in another country (*This may be either but will depend on whether the recipient has access to e-mail or not.*)

Lesson development

• **Introduction** Read the facts about e-mails and draw out some implications, e.g. the lack of confidentiality. Discuss other positive and negative facts about e-mails, e.g. you can send blind copies, you can get an instant response, you can prioritize messages, you can send attachments, people send too many e-mails as it is so easy to do.

• **Chain e-mail** This e-mail is like a chain letter. Such e-mails are a nuisance as they block up mail boxes and may contain viruses. Traditionally, chain letters create a psychological pressure on the reader because they claim it's unlucky to break the chain. Discuss the pressure in this e-mail, i.e. the mention of the charity.
This is a nuisance or 'spam' e-mail. Discuss the purposes of most spam, e.g to persuade people to do or buy something. Encourage students to question the e-mail. Possible questions might be:
  • Why did the writer send this?
  • What does the writer want the reader to do?
  • How does it try to persuade?

• **Netiquette** This term combines Inter**net** and **etiquette** and refers to safety and manners on the Internet. Read and discuss the netiquette rules, and complete activity 1 on safety and good manners.
Complete activities 2 and 3. Use **RS 3.3** as the framework for writing.
Other possible rules:
  – Tell a teacher or a parent if you receive an e-mail which makes you uncomfortable. *(safety)*
  – Do not believe everything you read online. *(safety)*
  – Never write hurtful things in an e-mail. *(manners)*
  – Do not forward chain letters or spam. *(manners)*

• **Plenary** Ask students to feed back one important rule for safety and one for good manners.

Extension ideas

• Discuss the persuasive techniques in the e-mail, e.g. calling the addressee 'friend', the repetition of the word 'help', imperatives such as 'Click' and 'Send'.

• Design a mouse mat or a screen saver which gives rules for Internet safety and/or manners.

Teaching support

Support could be directed at:
• prompting and questioning students on the tasks and discussions
• monitoring students' progress through the activities
• promoting extension tasks where appropriate.

Assessment

Encourage the students to complete the self-assessment sheet, **RS A**. In addition, **RSs B** and **C** can be used for peer and teacher assessment.

Viruses and hackers

Text type: Persuasive, Argument
Cross-curricular links: ICT

Assessment focuses:
Reading
AF3 Deduce, infer or interpret information, event or ideas from texts
AF6 Identify and comment on writers' purposes and viewpoints and the overall effect of the text on the reader

Learning objectives:
* To recognize persuasive techniques
* To understand that arguments are made up of both points for and against

Learning outcomes:
* To recognize how subject lines on e-mails can persuade you to open them
* To use arguments for and against hacking, in a role play

Framework objectives:
W1 Vowel choices
S&L13 Collaboration
S&L15 Explore in role
S&L16 Collaborate on scripts

Introduction

Ask students to turn to pages 32 and 33 in the Students' Book. Use the Introduction and Shared text to focus them on the unit topic. Ask them to find the spread about 'Viruses and hackers' in the Contents list. Focus on the English skills they will be using. You may wish to give students the self-assessment sheet (**RS A**), to fill in the learning objectives and outcomes.

Starter idea

RS 3.4 contains a series of arguments and counter arguments. Cut up some or all of the arguments, mix them up and give them to pairs of students. Ask them to match each argument with a counter argument.

Lesson development

* **Introduction** Introduce viruses by reading the main text on page 40 and do the first two activities. The missing letter, of course, is 'e'. You might point out that 'e' is the most frequently used letter in English. Talk about other frequently used letters, e.g. a, i, t, n, s. See AskOxford.com for useful information on letter and word frequency (www.askoxford.com/asktheexperts/faq/about words/frequency).

* **Subject lines** Q3 looks at how virus makers use subject lines in e-mails to entice readers into opening them. Draw out how they choose a subject which will intrigue a reader (e.g. as in the famous *I love you* virus), worry them (*Re: error, WARNING*) or make them feel it is serious and not to be ignored (*Important*). These are good examples of persuasive text, using very few words. Discuss how they exploit the readers' emotions.

* **Hacking** Read through the speech bubbles giving arguments about hacking and discuss the views. Pairs of students should use the views to help them create a role-play about hacking into the headteacher's computer: one is for and the other against. They may wish to make notes to help them remember their main arguments.

* **Plenary** Reuse the cards on **RS 3.4**, but this time only hand out the cards for one side of each argument. Ask students to think of a possible counter argument for as many cards as they can.

Extension ideas

* Think up other words and phrases that would work as an intriguing (e.g. Win £1000), worrying (e.g. Problem) or serious (e.g. Urgent!) subject line.
* Use the text on **RS 3.6** to explore the types of infection that affect computers, and how to persuade people to adopt anti-virus protection.

Teaching support

Support could be directed at:
* preparing the resources, e.g. the cards for the starters
* preparing a role-play with the teacher to model the technique for the students
* taping (audio or video) the role-plays for future assessment/evaluation.

Assessment

Encourage the students to complete the self-assessment sheet, **RS A**. In addition, **RSs B** and **C** can be used for peer and teacher assessment.

3 The Internet

Cyber stories

Text type: Fiction
Cross-curricular links: ICT

Assessment focuses:
Reading
AF2 Understand, describe, select or retrieve information, events or ideas from texts
Writing
AF1 Write imaginative, interesting and thoughtful texts
AF2 Write appropriate to task, reader and purpose

Learning objectives:
• To explore how fiction writers hold the interest of readers

Learning outcomes:
• To read, understand and form opinions on a selection of story openings and blurbs
• To continue writing one story extract

Framework objectives:
R17 Independent reading
Wr5 Story structure
Wr9 Link writing and reading
S&L1 Clarify through talk

Introduction

Ask students to turn to pages 32 and 33 in the Students' Book. Use the Introduction and Shared text to focus them on the unit topic. Ask them to find the spread about 'Cyber stories' in the Contents list. Focus on the English skills they will be using. You may wish to give students the self-assessment sheet (**RS A**), to fill in the learning objectives and outcomes.

Starter idea

Play 'Story consequences'. Students work in groups of four. Each student is given a piece of paper with the first line of a story. (Use **RS 3.5** for suggested lines.) They then write the next line of the story. They turn over the top of the paper so that the first line cannot be seen and only their words are visible. On the teacher's signal, each student passes the paper on to the next. They then write the next line and so on. Finally, open up the pages and enjoy reading the stories.

Lesson development

• **Introduction** Read through the story extracts on page 42. Discuss the students' first impressions of the stories. Draw attention to the titles which give extra clues to the story content.
• **Blurbs** Ask students to match up the blurbs on page 43 to the extracts on page 42. (The Help box explains what a blurb is.) Guide them to look for more obvious clues (e.g. the same words used: *VIMS*), less obvious clues (e.g. ways of expressing similar ideas: *Hyperbrain and biggest*

brain) and more subtle links (e.g. a computer with *a life of its own* and a computer that was almost *staring back*).
• Allow students time to discuss Q2 and Q3, as well as make some predictions. Draw out the following:
  – the stories involve normal people - children and parents
  – it is the computers that are extraordinary
  – the danger element
  – the computers being in control
  – the stories are written in the first person, from the child's perspective.
• **Writing** Set the final task: writing the next part of the story. The Help box gives useful support. This section could be organized as a guided writing session (see below).
• **Plenary** Share some of the stories written, giving a constructive evaluation of what the students have done well and where the story might go next.

Extension idea

Encourage the students to write their own opening to a computer story.

Guided writing

This sequence may be helpful:
• Organize students in groups, possibly according to the story chosen
• Remind them of the objective
• Review the features of the stories (see above)
• Model/support the writing of the first sentence
• Give them time to work independently
• Review and evaluate.
See **RSs G** and **H** for notes and planning for guided work.

Teaching support

Support could be directed at:
• preparing the resources, e.g. the resources for the starters
• leading a guided group
• looking for work to be read out at the end.

Assessment

Encourage the students to complete the self-assessment sheet, **RS A**. In addition, **RSs B** and **C** can be used for peer and teacher assessment.

3 The Internet

Internet challenge

Introduction

This final section is designed to test word and sentence level skills. It gives students the opportunity to complete short tasks independently.

The skills are linked to other parts of the unit but the activities stand alone. Students do not need to look back at the rest of the unit, although you may wish to draw their attention to the links as you review their work.

There are two suggested approaches:
1. Students start at number 1 and work their way though the activities at their own pace. There are extension ideas for some of the activities for those students who may require them.
2. Allow students time to complete one activity and review it together before moving on to the next task. This may be more supportive to those students who have difficulty working independently.

Task 1

Focus: key subject spellings

The words are:
1. online
2. website
3. download
4. e-mail

Extension: Use each word precisely in a sentence.

Task 2

Focus: imperatives

The answers are:
- **Protect** your computer.
- **Do not open** suspicious e-mails.
- **Use** an anti-virus program.
- **Keep** copies of important files.

Extension: Create their own instructions, using imperatives, on how to open a computer file, or how to save a document.

Task 3

Focus: punctuation of a story
Here is a possible solution:
Hi! I'm Charlie. I should not be telling you this – I am a computer hacker. Don't tell anyone will you? I'm brilliant but I'm in danger!

If students have used alternative punctuation, discuss their choices.

Extension: Ask students to write three more sentences, using at least two different punctuation marks.

Task 4

Focus: noun phrases

There are no right answers here, so discuss the students' choices. If they have difficulty thinking of ideas, give them the following possibilities and ask them to replace one or two words.

He held the empty, cardboard box.
He held the dusty, wooden box.

She looked at the short, nasty e-mail.
She looked at the funny e-mail from her dad.

I had an exciting but dangerous idea.
I had an amazingly simple idea.

Assessment

RS D can be used for self- and teacher assessment of the work done on the unit challenge spreads.

Extended text

There is an extended text, linked to the unit topic, on **RS 3.6**. This can be used in a variety of ways to extend the students' skills and to engage them further.

4 Extreme sports

Action sport

Text type: Information
Cross-curricular links: PE

Assessment focuses:
Reading
    AF2 Understand, describe, select or retrieve information
Writing
    AF2 Produce texts which are appropriate to task, reader and purpose
    AF3 Organize and present whole texts effectively

Learning objectives:
• To read, understand and comment on specialist vocabulary and information

Learning outcomes:
• To be able to match text and images, and to 'read' a graph
• To be able to write a dictionary definition

Framework objectives:
    W21 Subject vocabulary
    R2 Extract information
    Wr10 Organize texts appropriately
    S&L12 Exploratory talk

Introduction

Ask students to turn to pages 46 and 47 in the Students' Book. Use the Introduction and Shared text to focus them on the unit topic. Ask them to find the spread about 'Action sport' in the Contents list. Focus on the English skills they will be using. You may wish to give students the self-assessment sheet (**RS A**), to fill in the learning objectives and outcomes.

Starter ideas

a) Ask students how many words they can make from the word *snowboarding*. This will help them to break down the word, making it less daunting.

b) Dictionary game: read out the definition from a school dictionary of a word relevant to the lesson, e.g. water, snow, bicycle. Ask students to guess the word.

Lesson development

• **Introduction** Read the main text and draw attention to the sports depicted. Help students to read the names of the sports in Q1, breaking down the words if necessary.

• Q1 – Match the names of the sports with the pictures.

• Q2 - Discuss the origins of the sports:
    – snowboarding is new (links with skiing, surfing and skateboarding)
    – paragliding is relatively new (a mix of parachuting and hang gliding)

– white-water rafting is relatively new, but with obvious links to canoeing
    – rock climbing is well established
    – extreme cycling is a new sport derived from an existing one.

• **Dictionary definition** Encourage students to write a clear, concise dictionary definition of *extreme sport*. Look at the example in the Help box (and in a dictionary if possible). Point out the structure of a definition:
    – headword
    – word class
    – plural
    – definition.
RS 4.1 gives a helpful structure for their writing.

• **Young people and extreme sports** Read the bar chart.

• Q4 – Ensure students know that the 'most popular' means the sport which most people are doing. Check they know how to read both axes - the labels and the scale.

• Q5 – Students now need to look for the smallest number. Draw out possible ideas for why the sport is unpopular, e.g. *no snow, no access to facilities, expense.*

• Q6 – They should apply their general knowledge to the graph, e.g. fashions in sport change, new sports become popular.

• Q7 – The answer is 1/10. Emphasize that the same information can be presented in different ways.

• **Plenary** Reverse the Dictionary game suggested as a starter idea: supply one of the words, and ask students to create a definition.

Extension ideas

• Read the advert for parachuting on **RS 4.6**. Create an advert for another extreme sport.

• Find out more information about one extreme sport. Wikipedia is a useful source http://en.wikipedia.org/wiki/Main_Page.

Teaching support

Support could be directed at:
• helping students to read texts, by pointing out key features
• typing up good examples of definitions for a display showing features of definitions.

Assessment

Encourage the students to complete the self-assessment sheet, **RS A**. In addition, **RSs B** and **C** can be used for peer and teacher assessment of learning.

4 Extreme sports

Be prepared

Text type: Information, Instructions
Cross-curricular links: PE

Assessment focuses:
Reading
    AF3 Deduce, infer or interpret information, events or
    ideas from texts
Writing
    AF3 Organize and present whole texts effectively
    AF4 Paragraphs and cohesion
    AF6 Write with technical accuracy of syntax and punctuation

Learning objectives:
• To deduce and infer information through reading texts
  and images
• To organize instructions effectively

Learning outcomes:
• To use the clues in texts and pictures to complete some
  sentences about an ice climber
• To organize clear instructions on how to skateboard

Framework objectives:
    S13d Stylistic conventions of instructions
    R8 Infer and deduce
    Wr13 Instructions and directions

Introduction

Ask students to turn to pages 46 and 47 in the Students' Book. Use the Introduction and Shared text to focus them on the unit topic. Ask them to find the spread 'Be prepared' in the Contents list. Focus on the English skills they will be using. You may wish to give students the self-assessment sheet (**RS A**), to fill in the learning objectives and outcomes.

Starter idea

Invite the students to be detectives investigating the disappearance of the climber in the picture. They must look carefully for clues. What can they deduce and infer about the climber? For example, is she young or old?/fit and healthy?/an experienced climber?

Lesson development

• **Introduction** Read the main text.
• Q1 – The climber is doing something challenging. Set the students the challenge of completing each of the sentences to explain the equipment. Possible answers include:
  – *A helmet … It protects the head from falling rocks or from damage in the event of a fall.*
  – *An ice axe will help you to dig into the ice for footholds.*
  – *Crampons on your boots help you to grip the ice.*
  – *Ropes … will save you if you fall.*

• Q2 – Encourage students to consider the types of fitness needed to be a climber, e.g. strong leg muscles, flexible fingers and good grip, suppleness, good lungs.
• **Practice and training** Read the text and look at the pictures.
• Q3 – Discuss the extreme sports that require good balance, e.g. surfing, snowboarding, windsurfing.
• Q4 – Discuss the skills needed by the skateboarder, e.g. determination, being fit and flexible, control of the board, timing.
• Q5 – Students should write out the instructions in the right order. Draw attention to the Help box and emphasize the importance of giving instructions in the right sequence. **RS 4.2** has the instructions in the right order. These can be cut up and sorted, or students can highlight the features of instructions flagged up in the Help box.
• **Plenary** Golden tips: ask students to give one tip to a detective about trying to infer or deduce things, as they did when assessing the climber in the starter activity, e.g.
  – look closely at the pictures
  – ask the question 'why' a lot
  – look for clues in words
  – make connections between things.

Extension idea

Write simple instructions for an action in a sport they know well, e.g. taking a football penalty, diving into a swimming pool.

Teaching support

Support could be directed at:
• scribing the class's ideas for the starter activity
• prompting students with the reading and writing activities.

Assessment

Encourage the students to complete the self-assessment sheet, **RS A**. In addition, **RSs B** and **C** can be used for peer and teacher assessment of learning.

4 Extreme sports

The rush

Text type: Description, Poetry
Cross-curricular links: PE

Assessment focuses:
Writing
  AF1 Write imaginative, interesting and thoughtful texts
  AF7 Select appropriate and effective vocabulary

Learning objectives:
• To produce descriptive, reflective and imaginative writing

Learning outcomes:
• To use descriptive words and sentences about a bungee jumper
• To write a poem, describing the experience of a bungee jumper

Framework objectives:
  Wr8 Visual and sound effects
  Wr19 Reflective writing
  S&L1 Clarify through talk
  S&L12 Exploratory talk

Introduction

Ask students to turn to pages 46 and 47 in the Students' Book. Use the Introduction and Shared text to focus them on the unit topic. Ask them to find the spread 'The rush' in the Contents list. Focus on the English skills they will be using. You may wish to give students the self-assessment sheet (**RS A**), to fill in the learning objectives and outcomes.

Starter idea

'Bungee' is a wonderful onomatopoeic word. Give students 30 seconds to explore as many different ways of saying it as they can. Repeat with other words, such as 'buzz' and 'rush'.

Lesson development

• **Introduction** Read the main text and draw attention to the definitions in the glossary. Give students time to look at and discuss the picture of the bungee jumper.
• Q1 – Draw attention to the adjectives and consider which best describe the jumper and why. Ask students to add words to the list.
• Q2 – Encourage the students to use the sentence starters in the Help box. Remind them to use their chosen words thoughtfully and precisely.
• **Extreme poetry** Introduce the second picture of the bungee jumper further into the jump.
• Q3 – consider how the man is feeling. Create a word bank of ideas on the board.
• Q4 – introduce the task: to write a poem based on the man's feelings. Use **RS 4.3** to aid planning.

– Create a word bank of ideas (refer to the adjectives in the book and the word bank you created on the board).
– Remind students of poetic techniques (see the Help box) and allow them to practise them.
– Combine words and ideas into a draft poem.
– Redraft, carefully considering structure (see Help box).
This session might be organized as a guided writing session (see below).
• **Plenary** Share some of the poems, reading aloud either whole poems or parts of them and commenting on the techniques and skills used.

Extension idea

Use ICT to enhance the meaning of the poems, e.g. stretching words in 'Word Art', centring words down the page to emulate the bungee rope, superimposing the words over a suitable picture.

Guided writing

This sequence and **RS 4.3** may be helpful for guided group work:
• Organize students in groups, possibly according to ability
• Remind them of the task
• Use the word bank already created (see Extreme poetry above) to make personal word banks
• Review the features of a poem (see Help box), model some of the techniques and encourage students to practise techniques in pairs
• Draft initial ideas
• Discuss effective structure, e.g. short lines
• Give time for independent redrafting
• Review and evaluate.
See **RSs G** and **H** for notes and planning for guided work.

Teaching support

Support could be directed at:
• leading a guided group
• looking for work to be read out
• supporting extension work.

Assessment

Encourage the students to complete the self-assessment sheet, **RS A**. In addition, **RSs B** and **C** can be used for peer and teacher assessment of learning.

4 Extreme sports

Lifestyle

Text type: Persuasive
Cross-curricular links: PE

Assessment focuses:
Writing
  AF2 Produce texts which are appropriate to task, reader and purpose
  AF3 Organize and present whole texts effectively, sequencing and structuring information, ideas and events
  AF7 Select appropriate and effective vocabulary

Learning objectives:
• To write using argument and persuasion

Learning outcomes:
• To write a persuasive letter to a teacher
• To create effective sporting slogans

Framework objectives:
  S13e Stylistic conventions of persuasion
  S15 Vary formality
  Wr15 Express a view
  S&L15 Explore in role

Introduction

Ask students to turn to pages 46 and 47 in the Students' Book. Use the Introduction and Shared text to focus them on the unit topic. Ask them to find the spread 'Lifestyle' in the Contents list. Focus on the English skills they will be using. You may wish to give students the self-assessment sheet (**RS A**), to fill in the learning objectives and outcomes.

Starter idea

Role-play. Put students into threes: **A**, **B** and **C**.
A must persuade **B** to do something (e.g. lend them £1, let them copy their homework). **B** is reluctant. **C** must observe, then report back how **A** tried to persuade **B** (i.e. the persuasive techniques they used, such as repetition, exaggeration, emotional appeal, etc.).

Lesson development

• **Introduction** Ask students to read the conversation between Mal and Jaz. Check understanding and pull out some of the arguments, e.g. it's more fun to play in a team, it's good to test your limits.
• Q1 – Discuss the arguments. Which points do they agree with and why? Encourage students to form opinions.
• **Letter** Ensure that students understand Q2. **RS 4.4** and the sequence below will support their planning.
  – Brainstorm arguments for and against on the board, e.g. For: *extreme sports will raise interest in sport*. Against: *extreme sports may lead to more injuries*

– Encourage students to adopt the arguments they favour.
– Remind students of persuasive techniques (see Help box) and allow them to practise them
– Draft ideas
– Revise, check and redraft.
See notes below on guided work.
• **Fashion** Encourage the students to be the experts with Q3, listing belts, baggy trousers, beanies (hats) etc. Discuss the effect of this style of dress.
• **Slang** Q4 focuses on slang words. Examples from surfing: '*stick*' = *surfboard*, '*wipe out*' = *falling off the board*, '*tube*' = *tunnel formed by wave*.
Examples from skateboarding: '*lamer*' = *someone no good at skating*, '*fakie*' = *riding the board backwards*, '*switchback*' = *180 degree turn*.
Can they add more? Discuss why the slang arises.
• **Slogans** Slogans encapsulate the culture of extreme sports. Discuss the slogans in the spread (Q5), and how they are persuasive. Then ask students to design their own (Q6).
• **Plenary** Ask students to present and explain the slogans they have designed.

Extension idea

Create a poster to promote an extreme sport.

Guided writing

This sequence and **RS 4.4** may support guided group work:
• Remind them of the audience, purpose and form of the writing.
• Brainstorm the arguments as a group (on a flipchart, maybe) and ask them to copy down arguments they agree with.
• Review the features of persuasive text (refer to the Help box), model some of the techniques and let them practise techniques in pairs.
• Draft initial ideas then review with individuals.
• Give time for independent redrafting.
See **RSs G** and **H** for notes and planning for guided work.

Teaching support

Support could be directed at:
• leading a guided group
• reading out the script with the teacher.

Assessment

Encourage the students to complete the self-assessment sheet, **RS A**. In addition, **RSs B** and **C** can be used for peer and teacher assessment of learning.

4 Extreme sports

Cliffhangers

Text type: Description, fiction and non-fiction
Cross-curricular links: PE

Assessment focuses:
Reading
    AF5 Explain and comment on writers' use of language
Writing
    AF1 Write imaginative, interesting and thoughtful texts
    AF7 Select appropriate and effective vocabulary

Learning objectives:
- To gain greater understanding of how stories are crafted to 'hook in' a reader

Learning outcomes:
- To read and comment on two story extracts which end with a 'cliffhanger'
- To write a story extract which has drama and excitement, and to plan the remainder of the story.

Framework objectives:
    R14 Language choices
    Wr5 Story structure
    Wr7 Narrative devices
    Wr9 Link writing and reading

Introduction

Ask students to turn to pages 46 and 47 in the Students' Book. Use the Introduction and Shared text to focus them on the unit topic. Ask them to find the spread 'Cliffhangers' in the Contents list. Focus on the English skills they will be using. You may wish to give students the self-assessment sheet (**RS A**), to fill in the learning objectives and outcomes.

Starter idea

Give pairs two minutes to talk about the ending of an episode of a soap opera or serial drama they have seen. *How did it end?* Share ideas, and discuss why serials often end on an exciting note.

Lesson development

- **Introduction** Read the main text and ensure students understand what 'cliffhanger' means.
- **Extract 1** Read the extract from *Touching the Void* and check students' understanding. Note this is a non-fiction autobiographical account, but it works in the same way as fiction.
- Q1 – Focus on language. Encourage students to find the words relating to emptiness, e.g. nothingness, nothing, no thoughts, gone away, and speed, e.g. faster, faster than thought, swooping speed. Discuss the effects of the words and how repeating the same idea in different ways can emphasize the feeling of speed and the lack of emotion.

- Q2 – Draw attention to how the author expresses the thought that he is going to die: *simple words to denote the inevitable end; a short sentence contrasts with the sentences earlier; the present tense gives immediacy; the apostrophe gives impact.*
- **Extract 2** Again, confirm understanding of the extract. For Q1, discuss the effect of the word 'Skullcrack', e.g. its onomatopoeic quality, the hardness and violence of the word, connotations with death and pain.
- **Writing** Students should write the next paragraph. **RS 4.5** and the following sequence may support the planning:
  - Choose the extract
  - Decide on the narrator (**I** or **he**)
  - Plan what happens to the person
  - How does the character feel and react?
  - What words will help to describe this?
- **Story plan** Allow the students time to discuss and plan how the story will develop and end.
- **Plenary** Share and comment on their plans for the rest of the story.

Extension idea

Write a definition of 'cliffhanger', and outline some typical cliffhangers they have read or seen on television. Create a cliffhanger display.

Guided writing

This sequence may be helpful:
- Remind students of the objective and of the conventions (see Help box).
- Model/support the writing of the first sentence.
- Allow time for independent work.
- Review and evaluate.

See **RSs G** and **H** for notes and planning for guided work.

Teaching support

Support could be directed at:
- helping students to read texts, by pointing out key features
- leading a guided group
- typing up good examples of definitions for display.

Assessment

Encourage the students to complete the self-assessment sheet, **RS A**. In addition, **RSs B** and **C** can be used for peer and teacher assessment of learning.

4 Extreme sports

Extreme sports challenge

Introduction

This final section is designed to test word and sentence level skills. It gives students the opportunity to complete short tasks independently.

The skills are linked to other parts of the unit but the activities stand alone. Students do not need to look back at the rest of the unit, although you may wish to draw their attention to the links as you review their work.

There are two suggested approaches:
1. Students start at number 1 and are allowed to work their way though the activities at their own pace. There are extension ideas for some of the activities for those students who may require them.
2. Allow students time to complete one activity and review it together before moving on to the next task. This may be more supportive to those students who have difficulty working independently.

Task 1

Focus: the Latin prefix *cent*

The answers are:
1. century = one hundred years
2. centimetre = one hundredth of a metre
3. centipede = an insect with many legs

Other words using the same prefix:
a. cent = a coin worth one hundredth of a dollar
b. centenary = a 100th anniversary
c. centigrade = a temperature scale where water boils at 100 degrees
d. centurion = an officer of the Roman army in charge of 100 men.

Note: Words with the prefix *centr* (e.g. centre, central) come from the Latin *centrum* meaning *centre*.

Extension: Investigate other Latin prefixes, e.g. *bi* (two) and *in* (not).

Task 2

Focus: adverbs

The answers are:
- silently
- endlessly
- suddenly.

Extension: Think of three more adverbs ending –ly.

Task 3

Focus: connectives for sequencing

The instructions should be completed as below:

Skateboarding tricks: the ollie

First, put your front foot on the middle of the board and your back foot on the back.
Second, bend your knees.
Then slam your back foot down hard.
At **the same time**, jump in the air and pull up your knees.
Finally, as you land, bend your knees.
Roll away!

Extension: List other connectives that can be used for sequencing, e.g. *to begin with, next, after, lastly, before.*

Task 4

Focus: sentencing and punctuation

There is no one right answer, of course. Here is a possible version. Use it as a starting point to discuss possible changes.

Will had done many bungee jumps. He had never felt scared before but this time he did. Really scared. Suddenly he knew what was wrong. It was the leg harness – it didn't feel tight. He panicked!

Comment on the words added and removed; the punctuation added; the short sentences; whether 'Really scared' is a proper sentence, etc.

Assessment

RS D can be used for self- and teacher assessment of the work done on the unit challenge spreads.

Extended text

There is an extended text, linked to the unit topic on **RS 4.6**. This can be used in a variety of ways to extend the students' skills and to engage them further.

5 The Black Death

Deadly news

Introduction

Ask students to turn to pages 60 and 61 in the Students' Book. Use the Introduction and Shared text to focus them on the unit topic. Ask them to find the spread about 'Deadly news' in the Contents list. Focus on the English skills they will be using. You may wish to give students the self-assessment sheet (**RS A**), to fill in the learning objectives and outcomes.

Starter ideas

a) Proofreading: ask students to list three things that a writer might check for when proofreading, e.g. spelling errors, punctuation errors, paragraphs, sense, accurate facts, typographical errors.

b) Play 'Catch out the teacher'. Write two or three sentences with deliberate errors. Ask students to spot the errors.

Lesson development

• **Introduction** Read the introductory text, the memo from the editor and draw attention to the images. Then read the draft report.

• **Editing**
Q1 – Ask students to check the spellings indicated in the first paragraph. Investigate the pattern of the mistake (*ea* spellings). Ask them to spot the *ea* word in the second paragraph ('spread'). Explore other words that follow this pattern, e.g. lead, read, bear.

• Discuss why reports use sub-headings, e.g. to break up the text, to guide the reader through it, to grab the reader's attention. Ask students to create a suitable sub-heading for the third paragraph of the report. To do so, they will need to read it carefully and to identify the main point. You may wish to give less confident students some options, e.g.
  – Black Death kills lots of people
  – Millions dead
  – One in three perished.

• The students' knowledge of maths will help them check the accuracy of the statistic in the third paragraph. The answer is 25 million.

• Discuss the merits of each image and what each would add to the report. Which would be most informative?/revealing?/dramatic? Students also need to add a caption to the picture. This should encapsulate the main point of the picture.

• **RS 5.1** has the text of the report reproduced with the changes made, so that students can check their own report against it and make comparisons on the choice of sub-heading.

• **Plenary** Ask each student to create a headline which sums up an important aspect of the lesson.

Extension idea

Add an additional paragraph to the report on a different aspect, for example, how people tried to stop the plague. Encourage students to undertake some independent research for this. You could recommend www.insecta-inspecta.com/fleas/bdeath/Stop.html

Teaching support

Support could be directed at:
• helping students to read texts and drawing attention to potential errors
• prompting students to identify the main points, by giving them alternatives.

Assessment

Encourage the students to complete the self-assessment sheet, **RS A**. In addition, **RSs B** and **C** can be used for peer and teacher assessment of learning.

5 The Black Death

Deadly pests

Introduction

Ask students to turn to pages 60 and 61 in the Students' Book. Use the Introduction and Shared text to focus them on the unit topic. Ask them to find the spread about 'Deadly pests' in the Contents list. Focus on the English skills they will be using. You may wish to give students the self-assessment sheet (**RS A**), to fill in the learning objectives and outcomes.

Starter idea

Play 'Wink murder'. Have some fun as you introduce the idea of looking carefully for evidence. One student is the detective, and leaves the classroom briefly while a murderer is chosen. It's easiest if the class sits in a circle, but not essential. The murderer kills the others by winking at them. The victims can die dramatically. It's up to the detective to discover the murderer before the whole class dies!

Lesson development

- **Introduction** Read the introductory text and the evidence from the rat, the flea and the germ.
- Q1 – Put students into pairs and give them time to discuss the evidence. Advise them to reread the evidence together, and to make notes on each of the three suspects.
- Q2 – The students now have to make a decision and to write a speech which analyses the evidence and puts a persuasive case for their view. Draw attention to the Help box.

RS 5.2 will support the structuring of ideas. It suggests giving three reasons, so encourage students to comment on the evidence of each of the three suspects. This session could be taught as a guided writing session (see below).

- **Plenary** Ask students to read their speeches, either to a small group or to the class. It may be appropriate to record their speeches using audio or video equipment so that you can appraise how they have used the evidence, concentrating in particular on the strengths.

Extension ideas

- Research further evidence to include in their speeches.
- Prepare a role-play in which the three suspects give their own views about who or what they think is responsible for the Black Death.

Guided writing

This sequence and **RS 5.2** may be helpful:
- Review the task.
- Recap on the evidence from the three suspects.
- Review the features of their speech (see Help box).
- Model and practise using certain techniques, e.g. giving a view followed by a reason.
- Draft an initial sentence with support.
- Promote independent redrafting.
- Review and evaluate.

See **RSs G** and **H** for notes and planning for guided work.

Teaching support

Support could be directed at:
- leading a guided group
- help with reading the evidence
- reading the speeches of those students who have difficulty reading aloud
- recording the speeches, using audio or video equipment.

Assessment

Encourage the students to complete the self-assessment sheet, **RS A**. In addition, **RSs B** and **C** can be used for peer and teacher assessment of learning.

5 The Black Death

The victim

Text type: Information, Recount
Cross-curricular links: History

Assessment focuses:
Reading
    AF2 Understand, describe, select or retrieve information,
    events or ideas from texts
    AF3 Deduce, infer or interpret information
Writing
    AF1 Write imaginative, interesting and thoughtful texts
    AF2 Produce texts which are appropriate to tasks, reader
    and purpose

Learning objectives:
- To use information, as well as infer and deduce points,
  from an information text
- To write a recount text

Learning outcomes:
- To infer and deduce the signs of the plague in a well-
  known nursery rhyme
- To write a diary describing a plague victim

Framework objectives:
    S13b Stylistic conventions of recount
    R2 Extract information
    R8 Infer and deduce
    Wr14 Evocative description

Introduction

Ask students to turn to pages 60 and 61 in the Students' Book. Use the Introduction and Shared text to focus them on the unit topic. Ask them to find the spread about 'The victim' in the Contents list. Focus on the English skills they will be using. You may wish to give students the self-assessment sheet (**RS A**), to fill in the learning objectives and outcomes.

Starter idea

Nursery rhymes: give students two minutes to list as many nursery rhymes as they can. Then discuss what nursery rhymes are for. *Are they just nonsense or is there ever any meaning behind them? Do they ever deal with horrible things (e.g.* think of the ending of *Oranges and Lemons)?* Some may be complete nonsense, but often names and real places hint that they refer to something in history (e.g. Dr Foster, London Bridge).

Lesson development

- **Introduction** read the main text describing the symptoms of bubonic plague.
- Q1 – Put students into pairs and ask them to look for evidence of the plague in the nursery rhyme. Prompt them with questions if necessary. For example, *What might we deduce the 'ring o' roses' is? What might we infer from the fact that people carry*

a *'pocketful of posies'* or *sweet-smelling flowers?* It may be helpful to use **RS 5.3** to allow students to annotate this short text. This will help them to focus their discussion and to make appropriate, text-centred notes.

- Q2 – Students now need to use the information about the plague to write a diary entry, describing someone who is suffering from the plague. Suggest that the diary might describe a relative or a friend. Draw attention to the ideas given in the Help box. This part of the lesson might be taught as a guided writing session (see below).
- **Plenary** Ask each student to read out one sentence from his or her diary which they feel makes good use of the information.

Extension idea

Look at another nursery rhyme and decide what might be deduced from it. This website may be helpful for exploring origins of rhymes: www.rhymes.org.uk.

Guided writing

This sequence may be helpful:
- Review the task.
- Recap on the information given about the symptoms and what they might include.
- Review the features of a diary (see Help box).
- Model and practise using certain techniques, e.g. expressing personal feelings.
- Draft initial sentence(s) with support.
- Promote independent redrafting.
- Review and evaluate.

See **RSs G** and **H** for notes and planning for guided work.

Teaching support

Support could be directed at:
- leading a guided group
- prompting students with ideas for the starter
- drawing attention to key parts of the text
- helping students select work for the plenary.

Assessment

Encourage the students to complete the self-assessment sheet, **RS A**. In addition, **RSs B** and **C** can be used for peer and teacher assessment of learning.

The Game of Death

Text type: Instructions
Cross-curricular links: History

Assessment focuses:
Reading
  AF2 Understand, describe, select or retrieve information, events or ideas from texts
  AF3 Deduce, infer or interpret information, events or ideas from texts
Writing
  AF2 Produce texts which are appropriate to tasks, reader and purpose
  AF3 Organize and present whole texts effectively

Learning objectives:
- To identify the main idea behind a game
- To use available information to write a set of rules that are tried and tested

Learning outcomes:
- Use discussion to decide on how a game about the Black Death should be played
- To complete a set of rules on how to play a game

Framework objectives:
  R6 Active reading
  R7 Identify main ideas
  Wr13 Instructions and directions
  S&L10 Report main points

Introduction

Ask students to turn to pages 60 and 61 in the Students' Book. Use the Introduction and Shared text to focus them on the unit topic. Ask them to find the spread about 'The Game of Death' in the Contents list. Focus on the English skills they will be using. You may wish to give students the self-assessment sheet (**RS A**), to fill in the learning objectives and outcomes.

Starter idea

Board games: ask students to think of any board games they have played (such as Monopoly, Snakes and Ladders, Cluedo) and to list the typical features of a board game, e.g. what you have to do to win, how you make progress, problems that occur, equipment needed. Share their ideas and thoughts about board games.

Lesson development

- **Introduction** Read the introductory text, and the partial rules of the Game of Death. Draw attention to the game itself and take some initial reactions about what sort of game it is.
- Q1 – With students in pairs or small groups, ask them to discuss how the game should be played. They might consider:

- how to win
- how to progress around the board
- what problems players face
- whether they think it will be easy to win this game.

- Q2 – Ask students to write a set of rules for the game. They can complete the ones given, or write their own. Remind them that the audience is people who do not know the game. The rules must be clear and easy to follow. Draw attention to the Help box.
- Those students who need extra support can use **RS 5.4** which provides a framework for writing.
- Q3 – Encourage students to test their rules by swapping them with each other and playing the game according to the written rules. As they play, they should note down any adjustments that need to be made to make the rules more successful.
- **Plenary** Ask pairs of students to create three bullet points giving advice on writing instructions, e.g. use imperatives, put them in the right order, keep them simple.

Extension idea

Extend their study into persuasive writing by asking students to produce promotional material for the game, e.g. a magazine advert, a radio advert, a letter to history teachers.

Teaching support

Support could be directed at:
- keeping discussion work focused on the task
- being alert to, and guiding students away from, potential problems with the game rules
- using students' work to create a display which gives guidance on how to write rules.

Assessment

Encourage the students to complete the self-assessment sheet, **RS A**. In addition, **RSs B** and **C** can be used for peer and teacher assessment of learning.

5 The Black Death

The Great Plague

Introduction

Ask students to turn to pages 60 and 61 in the Students' Book. Use the Introduction and Shared text to focus them on the unit topic. Ask them to find the spread about 'The Great Plague' in the Contents list. Focus on the English skills they will be using. You may wish to give students the self-assessment sheet (**RS A**), to fill in the learning objectives and outcomes.

Starter idea

Play 'Picture it'. Ask students to study the picture of London during the Great Plague (on page 70 of the Students' Book). After one minute, students must close their books. In pairs they should discuss everything they can remember from the picture. They should decide on one important piece of information gained from the picture and report this to the teacher.

Lesson development

• **Introduction** Read the introductory text, and the information on people's attempts to survive the Great Plague.

• Q1 – In pairs or small groups, students can discuss the reasons for, and the possible success of, the actions taken by people to stop the plague spreading.

• Q2 – After the discussion, ask students to put the ideas in order of effectiveness.
  – *Isolation of the victims may seem harsh, but would have helped to stop the spread of disease.*
  – *It was also a good idea to find and bury the dead.*
  – *Killing cats and dogs led to a rise in the rat population. This was bad news as rats were carriers.*
  – *The disease was not carried by air, so fires would make little difference.*
  – *Smoking would do nothing but harm.*

• Q3 – **Pepys' diary** Read the extracts from Pepys' diary and discuss what we learn. Use the Help box to prompt students' responses.

• Q4 – Students should write an advice leaflet on how to avoid the plague. They should imagine they are writing it in 1665, so do not have the benefit of knowing the actual causes. Draw attention to the Help box. Use **RS 5.5** if they need help with organization.

• **Plenary** 'Just 30 seconds': a game based on the Radio 4 game *Just a Minute*. Ask selected students to recount everything they have learned through their reading in this lesson in 30 seconds, without hesitation or repetition.

Extension ideas

• Read **RS 5.6** which contains an extract from a fictional diary relating a sad episode. Retell the episode in pictures, drama or verse.

• Research the story of the Great Plague. A useful source is: www.channel4.com/history/microsites/H/history/plague.

Teaching support

Support could be directed at:
• keeping discussion focused on the task
• supporting students with writing by modelling and prompting ideas.

Assessment

Encourage the students to complete the self-assessment sheet, **RS A**. In addition, **RSs B** and **C** can be used for peer and teacher assessment of learning.

The Black Death challenge

Introduction

This final section is designed to test word and sentence level skills. It gives students the opportunity to complete short tasks independently.

The skills are linked to other parts of the unit but the activities stand alone. Students do not need to look back at the rest of the unit, although you may wish to draw their attention to the links as you review their work.

There are two suggested approaches:
1. Students start at number 1 and are allowed to work their way though the activities at their own pace. There are extension ideas for some of the activities for those students who may require them.
2. Allow students time to complete one activity and review it together before moving on to the next task. This may be more supportive to those students who have difficulty working independently.

Task 1

Focus: plurals

The answers are:
1. child – children
2. woman – women
3. foot – feet
4. mouse – mice
5. bacterium – bacteria.

Other irregular plurals they may find are:
- man – men
- tooth – teeth
- goose – geese
- fungus – fungi.

Task 2

Focus: apostrophes

The answers are:
1. a (I **a**m)
2. i (he **i**s)
3. wi (she **wi**ll)
4. o (do n**o**t)
5. o (could n**o**t)

Extension: Think of three more words where we commonly use apostrophes to show missing letters. (For example, *didn't, it's, we've, haven't, they'll*)

Task 3

Focus: connectives to show cause and effect

The most appropriate responses are:

*Rats live near humans **so** they can eat their food and waste. The flea is sick **because** it has bacteria in its stomach. Humans grow ill **because** a flea bites them.*

Extension: List other connectives that can be used to show cause and effect, e.g. *as a result of, therefore, since, until, as long as, whenever, consequently, so that.*

Task 4

Focus: alphabetical order and codes

The answer is:
One day I will rule the world!

Extension:
- Create another message using this code.
- Create another code based on the alphabet.

Assessment

RS D can be used for self- and teacher assessment of the work done on the unit challenge spreads.

Extended text

There is an extended text, linked to the unit topic on **RS 5.6**. This can be used in a variety of ways to extend the students' skills and to engage them further.

6 Crime

The law

Text type: Information, Explanation
Cross-curricular links: Citizenship

Assessment focuses:
Reading
AF2 Understand, describe, select or retrieve information, events or ideas from texts
AF3 Deduce, infer or interpret information, events or ideas from texts
Writing
AF6 Write with technical accuracy of syntax and punctuation

Learning objectives:
• To explore, through reading and talking, where and why we have rules

Learning outcomes:
• To identify and comment on some offences shown in a picture
• To find out about laws affecting young people

Framework objectives:
W1 Vowel choices
R2 Extract information
Wr12 Develop logic
S&L1 Clarify through talk

Introduction

You may wish to open the lesson with the starter idea (see below). Then ask students to turn to pages 74 and 75 in the Students' Book. Use the Introduction and Shared text to focus them on the unit topic. Ask them to find the spread about 'The law' in the Contents list. Focus on the English skills they will be using. You may wish to give students the self-assessment sheet (**RS A**), to fill in the learning objectives and outcomes.

Starter idea

Ask students to supply the missing word (law) in each of these phrases:
> The _____ of the jungle.
> Letter of the _____.
> Strong arm of the _____.
> A _____ unto itself.

Discuss the exact meaning of each expression. Ask students if they know more expressions or words containing the word 'law', e.g. mother-in-law, law of the land, law and order.

Lesson development

• **Introduction** The introductory text and pictures, together with the first three activities, should stimulate thought on where and why we use rules.
• Q1 – Answers are: school, games, driving a car
• Q2 – Ask small groups to discuss what would happen if there were no rules in these situations (allocate one situation per group). Share and compare ideas.

• Q3 – Brainstorm other areas of life subject to rules, e.g. families, clubs, hospitals, work, pubs.
• **Law and Crimes** Q4 – Challenge students to find as many of the crimes as possible in the picture. The Help box will direct them to the right areas:
  – *Parking on zigzag lines*
  – *Dropping litter*
  – *Being drunk and disorderly*
  – *Cycling on the pavement*
  – *Damaging public property*
  – *Not stopping at a zebra crossing*
  – *Breaking into a car and stealing*
  – *Drinking and driving*
  – *Leaving dog mess on the pavement*
  Students can use **RS 6.1** to annotate the picture, identifying the offences, with brief explanations.
• Q5 – Encourage discussion and opinions about which is the worst crime depicted. You could use the Help Box to match crimes to categories or put the crimes in rank order. Ask students to explain their decisions. Finally use the sentence structure provided to construct a written opinion.
• **Laws and young people** Q6 - The ages are a) thirteen, b) sixteen, c) seven, d) seventeen, e) eighteen, f) fourteen.
• Q7 – Other laws linked to age, affect:
  – leaving school (16)
  – getting married (18, or 16 with parental consent)
  – buying a lottery ticket (16)
  – buying beer with a meal in a pub or restaurant (16)
  The Connexions Direct website has a full list (www.connexionsdirect.com/index.cfm?pid=161&catalogueContentID=176).
• **Plenary** Write a ten-word sentence saying why rules or laws are helpful.

Extension idea

Write a short explanation for one of the laws affecting young people (e.g. part-time jobs).

Teaching support

Support could be directed at:
• supporting and prompting student talk activities
• making notes from students' discussions to help them feed back to the rest of the group.

Assessment

Encourage the students to complete the self-assessment sheet, **RS A**. In addition, **RSs B** and **C** can be used for peer and teacher assessment of learning.

6 Crime

Youth crime

Text type: Information
Cross-curricular links: Citizenship, Maths

Assessment focuses:
Reading
AF2 Understand, describe, select or retrieve information, events or ideas from texts
AF4 Identify and comment on the structure and organization of texts
Writing
AF3 Organize and present whole texts effectively

Learning objectives:
• To understand and explain what a range of texts tells us about young people and crime

Learning outcomes:
• To identify how information can be presented in different ways, including graphs
• To explore the meaning and effects of anti-social behaviour, through talk and writing

Framework objectives:
R7 Identify main ideas
R11 Print, sound and image
Wr10 Organize texts appropriately
Wr12 Develop logic

Introduction

Ask students to turn to pages 74 and 75 in the Students' Book. Use the Introduction and Shared text to focus them on the unit topic. Ask them to find the spread about 'Youth crime' in the Contents list. Focus on the English skills they will be using. You may wish to give students the self-assessment sheet (**RS A**), to fill in the learning objectives and outcomes.

Starter idea

Give students the following list of words: *antifreeze, anti-aircraft, anticlockwise.*
Ask them:
a) the meaning of the prefix anti- (*against, preventing*)
b) to list other words using the same prefix (e.g. antibiotic, anticlimax, antiseptic).
Challenge them to look out for the same prefix later in the lesson (*antisocial*).

Lesson development
• **Introduction** Through the introductory text and Q1, explore the idea of criminal responsibility. Prompt discussion with comments such as: *It is a heavy responsibility. Does a 10 year-old have other such responsibilities? Between 10 and 14, children can be convicted if it's proved they know they were doing something seriously wrong. At 14, young people are considered fully responsible. What are the differences between a 10 and a 14 year-old?*

• Q2 – This activity encourages students to see how the same information can be presented in different ways, i.e. as written text or a graphic. Point out which are the pie charts and which is the bar chart.
• Q3 – By sketching out the graphs and adding the labels, students need to consider the clarity of the content and the needs of the reader.
• Q4 – Discuss what is gained by presenting information in the form of a graph. Ask students which method of presentation they find easiest to understand.
• **ASBOs** Read the text and discuss what they know about ASBOs. Talk about where and when offences happen, as well the effects of such behaviour. Emphasize how the effects might be exacerbated for different people, e.g. elderly, young children, people on their own.
• Students can write up their ideas, copying out the table or using **RS 6.2**. This RS also has space for them to suggest other types of behaviour, e.g. inconsiderate parking, late-night parties, fireworks at unexpected times, cycling on the pavement.
• **Plenary** Ask students to produce a simple graph or table on one aspect of the lesson, e.g.
  – how much reading, talking, writing they did
  – how many activities they completed
  – what they think are the worst types of antisocial behaviour.

Extension idea

Do some research, using information books (preferably on crime) to investigate other ways to organize and present statistical information.

Teaching support

Support could be directed at:
• prompting student talk activities
• playing 'devil's advocate' in talk tasks to encourage students to explain their ideas
• modelling how to sketch out graphs and label them clearly.

Assessment

Encourage the students to complete the self-assessment sheet, **RS A**. In addition, **RSs B** and **C** can be used for peer and teacher assessment of learning.

6 Crime

Crime then and now

Text type: Report
Cross-curricular links: Citizenship

Assessment focuses:
Reading
  AF3 Deduce, infer or interpret information, events or
  ideas from texts
  AF5 Explain and comment on writers' use of language,
  including grammatical and literary features at word and
  sentence level

Learning objectives:
• To compare newspaper reports on crimes past and present

Learning outcomes:
• To study the language and content of news reports
• Identify the common features of newspaper reports

Framework objectives:
  R7 Identify main ideas
  R8 Infer and deduce
  R10 Media audiences
  S&L1 Clarify through talk

Introduction

Ask students to turn to pages 74 and 75 in the Students' Book. Use the Introduction and Shared text to focus them on the unit topic. Ask them to find the spread about 'Crime then and now' in the Contents list. Focus on the English skills they will be using. You may wish to give students the self-assessment sheet (**RS A**), to fill in the learning objectives and outcomes.

Starter idea

Give students two of the headlines in the spread, one old and one recent. Ask pairs of students to decide:
• where the writing is from
• what the text might be about.

Lesson development

• **Introduction** Read through the newspaper reports on the double-page spread, drawing attention to the Glossary box to explain unfamiliar vocabulary.
• Q1 – Ideally, pair up students and ask them to look for evidence, before reporting back.
  – Extract 1 is from the *Daily News*, 27 November 1918
  – Extract 2 is from the *Guardian*, 8 January 2002
  – Extract 3 is from the *Daily News* 28 May 1886
  – Extract 4 is from BBC News online, 29 July 2005
• Q2 – Comparing the reports might be undertaken as a guided reading session (see below). **RS 6.3** may be used to record findings. You may wish to draw out these language points:

– old-fashioned words like 'lad' and 'prisoner', where today we might use 'youth' and 'defendant'
– outdated expressions, such as 'beastly drunk' and 'acted like a madman'. Compare these with references to 'young people' and 'binge drinking' in the modern reports
– the punctuation of the headlines: the modern reports contrast with the old ones, by using capital letters only at the start of the headline.
Some points on content:
– 'Birched', 'reformatory', 'tramcar' and 'hard labour' refer to old ideas, while 'mobile phone theft' and 'buses' are modern
– More statistics occur in the modern reports, e.g. 'up to half a million…', whilst the older reports feature more opinion e.g. 'he acted like a madman'.
• Q3 – Draw attention to the Help box for support and ideas.
• **Plenary** Ask students to write a suitable short headline about this lesson, e.g. 'Times change, crimes don't' 'Students spot old-fashioned language'

Extension idea

Extend the research into old newspaper reports by looking at reports from the British Library online archive: www.uk.olivesoftware.com.

Guided reading

This sequence may be helpful:
• Remind students of the objective – to compare texts.
• Review what they are looking for: features of language and content.
• Allow pairs time to read and make notes.
• As a group, discuss their findings.
• Write up notes individually.
• Review what they have learned.
See **RSs G** and **H** for notes and planning for guided work.

Teaching support

Support could be directed at:
• helping the reading of the texts
• leading a guided group
• assisting extension work.

Assessment

Encourage the students to complete the self-assessment sheet, **RS A**. In addition, **RSs B** and **C** can be used for peer and teacher assessment of learning.

6 Crime

In court

Text type: Information, Explanation
Cross-curricular links: Citizenship

Assessment focuses:
Reading
    AF2 Understand, describe, select or retrieve information,
    events or ideas from texts
    AF3 Deduce, infer or interpret information, events or
    ideas from texts
Writing
    AF2 Write appropriate to tasks, reader and purpose

Learning objectives:
• To use role-play to support joint decision making

Learning outcomes:
• In role, as a magistrate, to take decisions on possible crimes
• To write an explanation of the decisions made.

Framework objectives:
    R2 Extract information
    Wr12 Develop logic
    S&L13 Collaboration
    S&L15 Explore in role

Introduction

Ask students to turn to pages 74 and 75 in the Students' Book. Use the Introduction and Shared text to focus them on the unit topic. Ask them to find the spread about 'In court' in the Contents list. Focus on the English skills they will be using. You may wish to give students the self-assessment sheet (**RS A**), to fill in the learning objectives and outcomes.

Starter idea

Play 'Decisions': working in threes, two students have to make decisions on something (e.g. planning a birthday party, redesigning the classroom, planning a holiday). They have only two minutes. The third student times the discussion and is the observer – noting down positive behaviour (e.g. asking questions, praising the others' ideas, keeping on task) and negative features (e.g. going off task, not listening, not compromising). Take feedback from the observer on the positives and negatives (without mentioning names!).

Lesson development

• **Introduction** Read the introductory text. Ensure students understand the job of a magistrate. Check too that they understand the three cases given, but do not ask for their opinions about them at this stage.

• Q1 to 4 – Outline and support the role-play:
    – *Acting as a panel of magistrates, they have three cases to decide on in this session.*
    – *They must use the information on page 83 to help them.*
    – *Give them time to read, talk and make notes.*
    – *Prompt them to write down their final decisions, with reasons.*
    – *Listen to and discuss their verdicts.*
    RS 6.4 may be used to provide a structure for their notes and decisions. If the students read the notes they will discover that each young person is probably committing an offence.

• Q5 – Organize this activity as in the Students' Book. Alternatively, have half of the groups remain as magistrates and half becoming the young people.

• The magistrates should list all the questions that they would like to ask the young people. The young people must try to come up with convincing reasons for their actions.

• Each group of magistrates must join up with a group of young people. Conduct a role-play where the magistrates question the young people. Ask the students whether the questioning would make any difference to their original decisions.

• **Plenary** Have a class vote, through a show of hands, on whether each young person has committed an offence. Discuss the results. Ask students to finish this sentence: *In order to make a joint decision, it's important to...*

Extension idea

Encourage the students to continue the role-play, making further decisions on what they think should happen to each of the young people.

Teaching support

Support could be directed at:
• supporting and prompting student talk activities
• modelling (with the teacher) good discussion and decision-making skills in front of the class
• videoing the role-plays, in order to replay and discuss the decision making.

Assessment

Encourage the students to complete the self-assessment sheet, **RS A**. In addition, **RSs B** and C can be used for peer and teacher assessment of learning.

6 Crime

Words from inside

Text type: Poem, Argument
Cross-curricular links: Citizenship

Assessment focuses:
Reading
    AF2 Understand, describe, select or retrieve information, events or ideas from texts
    AF4 Identify and comment on the structure and organization of texts
Writing
    AF1 Write imaginative, interesting and thoughtful texts
    AF2 Produce texts which are appropriate to tasks, reader and purpose

Learning objectives:
• To use reading and talking to help form views and arguments about the topic of prison

Learning outcomes:
• To read, understand and appreciate a prisoner's poem
• To form views on the good and bad points of prisons

Framework objectives:
R12 Character, setting and mood
R14 Language choices
Wr15 Express a view
S&L1 Clarify through talk

Introduction

Ask students to turn to pages 74 and 75 in the Students' Book. Use the Introduction and Shared text to focus them on the unit topic. Ask them to find the spread about 'Words from inside' in the Contents list. Focus on the English skills they will be using. You may wish to give students the self-assessment sheet (**RS A**), to fill in the learning objectives and outcomes.

Starter idea

To focus students on the fact that many things have good and bad sides, play a game of 'Fortunately, unfortunately'. Go around the class, with one person giving a positive statement; the next a negative and so on. For example:

> *Fortunately, I was on time for school this morning.*
> *Unfortunately, my tutor wasn't.*
> *Fortunately, no one minded.*
> *Unfortunately, the Headteacher did…*

Lesson development

• **Introduction** Read the poem 'It's humans that they put in prison'. Try experimenting with reading it in different ways. For example,
    – the whole class reading it together
    – reading around the class, with one word per person
    – as above with one line per person.

• Q1 – In this activity, bring out the contrast in human and animal behaviour. What would the students expect human (and animal) behaviour to be like?

• Q2 and 3 – Focus on the structure of the poem. The repeated words 'humans', 'animals' and 'prison' bring together the key ideas. As the lines grow longer, so Eddie S builds his argument.

• Explore the tone or voice of the poem. There is a childlike simplicity to the words. Ask students how this makes us feel sympathy. How does the writer feel – angry, sad or amused?

• Q4 – Encourage students to use their knowledge of the patterns of the poem, e.g. the repetition, the building of the argument. Encourage thought and imagination too, e.g. the use of a question.

• **Ryan** Q5 to 8 – Ask students to read the transcript – reading up to a punctuation mark before another student takes over, and so on. Discuss what Ryan has learned, e.g. the advice, the contacts, the 'bigger and better ways'. Consider the changes he's undergone, and what 'changed' means in the first line of the transcript.

• Direct students to the Help box for ideas for the writing. Use **RS 6.5** to help scaffold their writing, if necessary.

• **Plenary** Ask students to choose one word that sums up what they have read about in this lesson. Answers might include *prison, punishment, behaviour, anger.*

Extension ideas

• Discuss what can be done to prevent people like Ryan from reoffending.

• Read the extended text on **RS 6.6** for a different viewpoint: 'A day in the life of a prison officer'. What points does the prison officer make?

Teaching support

Support could be directed at:
• helping with the reading of the texts
• leading a guided group
• assisting with extension work.

Assessment

Encourage the students to complete the self-assessment sheet, **RS A**. In addition, **RSs B** and **C** can be used for peer and teacher assessment of learning.

6 Crime

Crime challenge

Introduction

This final section is designed to test word and sentence level skills. It gives students the opportunity to complete short tasks independently.

The skills are linked to other parts of the unit but the activities stand alone. Students do not need to look back at the rest of the unit, although you may wish to draw their attention to the links as you review their work.

There are two suggested approaches:
1. Students start at number 1 and are allowed to work their way though the activities at their own pace. There are extension ideas for some of the activities for those students who may require them.
2. Allow students time to complete one activity and review it together before moving on to the next task. This may be more supportive to those students who have difficulty working independently.

Task 1

Focus: proper nouns

Here is the passage with the capital letters restored.

> There are many stories about detectives. **S**herlock **H**olmes is a well-known detective. **S**herlock dresses in a deerstalker hat and cape. He lives in **B**aker **S**treet, in **L**ondon.
>
> **M**iss **M**arple is a little old lady. She is nosy and clever. **H**ercule **P**oirot is a smart detective. He comes from **B**elgium.

Extension: Write out the names of three more detectives (from book or screen), putting capital letters in the right places.

Task 2

Focus: slang

Here are the slang words matched with the formal versions.

Slang	Formal
porky pies	lies
tea leaf	thief
cop shop	police station
cough up	confess, own up
the nick	prison

Task 3

Focus: bullet points

- Know the IMEI number of your phone.
- If your phone is stolen, give the IMEI number to the police.
- To find the IMEI number, dial ★ # 0 6 #.
- Keep your phone out of sight in public places.

Extension: Create a bullet-point list on how to keep bicycles safe.

Task 4

Focus: slogans

The full English version of the slogan is:
Lock it, Mark it, Keep it, Use it, Don't Lose it!

Extension: Create another text slogan, e.g. for stopping people dropping litter or doing graffiti.

Assessment

RS D can be used for self- and teacher assessment of the work done on the unit challenge spreads.

Extended text

There is an extended text, linked to the unit topic on **RS 6.6**. This can be used in a variety of ways to extend the students' skills and to engage them further.

7 Fashion

Fashion is...

Text type: Information
Cross-curricular links: Art

Assessment focuses:
Reading
   AF3 Deduce, infer or interpret information, event or ideas
   from texts
Writing
   AF4 Construct paragraphs and display cohesion within and
   between paragraphs
   AF5 Vary sentences for clarity, purpose and effect

Learning objectives:
• To use text and talk to explore what we mean by the
  term 'fashion'

Learning outcomes:
• To discuss and makes notes on some images and
  comments on fashion
• To write a paragraph about what fashion is

Framework objectives:
  R4 Note-making
  R8 Infer and deduce
  Wr11 Present information
  S&L1 Clarify ideas

Introduction

Ask students to turn to pages 88 and 89 in the Students' Book. Use the Introduction and Shared text to focus them on the unit topic. Ask them to find the spread entitled 'Fashion is...' in the Contents list. Focus on the English skills they will be using. You may wish to give students the self-assessment sheet (**RS A**), to fill in the learning objectives and outcomes.

Starter idea

Play fashion 'Pictionary'. Split the class into two groups. Write the names of a number of fashion items or trends (e.g. poncho, skate belt, trainers, tattoos, flares) on slips of paper. Give one slip to one student. They must draw a picture of the item for their group, who gain a point for a correct guess. If the guess is wrong, the opposing team can guess it and try to gain the point. The first team to reach five points wins.

Lesson development

• **Introduction** Use the introductory text and pictures to initiate discussion on what fashion is.
• Q1 – Ask students to talk and make notes about the pictures on the page. You might also want to bring up the idea of stereotyping, and why this can be dangerous. Students can use **RS 7.1** to collate their notes about the pictures.

• Q2 – Use the ideas and statements about fashion on page 91 as a starting point to discuss their own ideas about fashion. Which statements do they agree or disagree with? What statements or ideas of their own do they have? Again, encourage the students to use **RS 7.1** to record their ideas.
• Q3 – Students can now present their own ideas on fashion. They should explain what fashion is and perhaps give their own views about fashion. This session may be suitable for guided writing (see below).
• Encourage students to put ideas into their own words. Advise them not to start each sentence in the same way, e.g. 'Fashion is...' but to vary sentence openings, e.g. 'The good side of fashion is...', 'I think that...'. If they have been using **RS 7.1**, this can prompt their ideas.
• **Plenary** Ask students to swap their writing with a partner. They should pick out one good point from their partner's work and share this with the rest of the class.

Extension idea

Choose one of the pictures and write a description of the fashion depicted.

Guided writing

This sequence may be helpful:
• Review the task.
• Recap on the information.
• Review the requirements of the text – part explanation, part opinion.
• Model and practise using certain techniques, e.g. starting sentences in different ways.
• Draft initial sentence(s) with support.
• Allow time for individual writing.
See **RSs G** and **H** for notes and planning for guided work.

Teaching support

Support could be directed at:
• leading a guided group
• typing up good examples of writing about fashion for a display
• helping students to select points for the plenary.

Assessment

Encourage the students to complete the self-assessment sheet, **RS A**. In addition, **RSs B** and **C** can be used for peer and teacher assessment of learning.

7 Fashion

Fashion over time

Text type: Information
Cross-curricular links: Art, History

Assessment focuses:
AF3 Deduce, infer or interpret information, events or ideas from texts
Writing
AF6 Write with technical accuracy of syntax and punctuation in phrases, clauses and sentences

Learning objectives:
• To use information from a timeline to find out about fashion over the years

Learning outcomes:
• To study a timeline on fashion, and make deductions about the people depicted
• To write an addition to the timeline

Framework objectives:
R1 Locate information
R8 Infer and deduce
Wr11 Present information

Introduction

Ask students to turn to pages 88 and 89 in the Students' Book. Use the Introduction and Shared text to focus them on the unit topic. Ask them to find the spread about 'Fashion over time' in the Contents list. Focus on the English skills they will be using. You may wish to give students the self-assessment sheet (**RS A**), to fill in the learning objectives and outcomes.

Starter idea

Ask students to create a simple timeline, e.g. every hour since 8 am this morning. The timeline should have regular divisions of time, and students should label significant points, e.g. registration, lunchtime. Make the point that timelines can help us to break down periods of time into recognizable chunks.

Lesson development

• **Introduction** Draw attention to the timeline on pages 92 and 93 in the Students' Book. Explain that it covers 500 years and so it only highlights a limited number of fashions. Give students time to explore the fashions, e.g. what they recognize, what they like and dislike.
• Q1 – Students must decide on the missing picture for the 1920s. It is picture B. Encourage students to give reasons for their choice.
• Q2 – With the aid of the Help box, ask students to consider the effects of the clothes. Encourage them to imagine what it must be like to actually wear the clothes and how they would affect the person's life.

• Q3 – Students need to sum up their thoughts about each picture in just one sentence. Again, ask for the reasoning behind their comments, e.g. *The clothes of the Georgians look grand and expensive, and I think these are rich people. I think that the large wigs show they want to impress others.*
RS 7.2 may be used as a frame for their writing.
• Q4 – In imagining the fashions of the future, students can be really imaginative and inventive. Remind them of the changes that have taken place over the last hundred years, before they look forward and attempt to predict future changes. Advise them, too, that aspects of fashion often repeat themselves so it needn't be totally original. They can also think up names for their creations.
• **Plenary** Share some of the ideas they have created in Q4.
• Ask each student to consider which past fashion looked at in the lesson they would like to try, and why. (They must choose one.)

Extension ideas

• Find out more about one of the fashions looked at in the lesson.
• Find another fashion to add to the timeline, e.g. the Regency period (of Jane Austen), or the mods and mini skirts of the 1960s.

Teaching support

Support could be directed at:
• help with reading and discussion
• encouraging students to explain their ideas
• ensuring that students write in full sentences for Q3
• researching suitable books/websites for extension tasks.

Assessment

Encourage the students to complete the self-assessment sheet, **RS A**. In addition, **RSs B** and **C** can be used for peer and teacher assessment of learning.

7 Fashion

Blue jeans

Text type: Quiz, Opinions
Cross-curricular links: Design and technology, Art

Assessment focuses:
Reading
  AF3 Deduce, infer or interpret information, events or
  ideas from texts
Writing
  AF4 Construct paragraphs and display cohesion within
  and between paragraphs

Learning objectives:
- To use the subject of jeans to a) sharpen deduction skills, and b) to establish a point of view

Learning outcomes:
- To create the questions that fit with a list of answers about jeans
- To write a paragraph expressing a view about jeans

Framework objectives:
  R8 Infer and deduce
  Wr15 Express a view
  Wr16 Validate an argument

Introduction

Ask students to turn to pages 88 and 89 in the Students' Book. Use the Introduction and Shared text to focus them on the unit topic. Ask them to find the spread about 'Blue jeans' in the Contents list. Focus on the English skills they will be using. You may wish to give students the self-assessment sheet (**RS A**), to fill in the learning objectives and outcomes.

Starter idea

Play '5 Ws'. Give students a topic and ask them to think of a question beginning with *what, why, when, where* and *who*. For example:
Topic – snakes
- What is the biggest snake?
- Why do many people fear snakes?
- When do snakes sleep?
- Where are snakes found in Britain?
- Who can have a pet snake?

Lesson development

- **Introduction** Read through the quiz answers on jeans, emphasizing that these have been written in response to 'unseen' questions.
- Q1 – Allow pairs of students time to discuss possible questions that would elicit these answers. You may wish to model how to work out the first one: *What are jeans made from?*
- Q2 – Tell students you would like them to write down a plausible question for each answer. Refer them to the Help box.

- Use **RS 7.3** with students who will have difficulty with the task. The questions are on the RS and students must match them with the answers.
- **Will jeans always be popular?** This may organized as a guided writing task (see below). Read through the opinions on page 95. Do they strongly agree or disagree with any of the points? Why? Give students time to exchange views in pairs or small groups. The Help box provides a structure for their discussion.
- Ask students to write a paragraph on their views. Again, prompt the use of the Help box.
- **Plenary** Play 'What is the question?' Give pairs an answer relating to something from the lesson, e.g. denim, baggy, indigo. Allow 20 seconds to collaborate on the question. Award points for the best or most entertaining questions.

Extension idea

Design a questionnaire about jeans. Compose a set of between five and ten questions that will ascertain the views of friends and family about the subject of jeans.

Guided writing

This sequence may be helpful:
- Review the task.
- Read through the opinions and discuss them.
- Review the requirements of the text – one paragraph, giving a viewpoint.
- Model expressing a view in writing.
- Draft initial sentence(s) with support.
- Allow time for individual writing.
See **RSs G** and **H** for notes and planning for guided work.

Teaching support

Support could be directed at:
- leading a guided group
- helping with writing out questions
- modelling, with the teacher, an answer and question for the plenary.

Assessment

Encourage the students to complete the self-assessment sheet, **RS A**. In addition, **RSs B** and **C** can be used for peer and teacher assessment of learning.

7 Fashion

Fashion victims

Text type: Information, Recount
Cross-curricular links: Citizenship, Maths

Assessment focuses:
Reading
  AF2 Understand, describe, select or retrieve information, events or ideas from texts
  AF3 Deduce, infer or interpret information, events or ideas from texts
Writing
  AF1 Write imaginative, interesting and thoughtful text

Learning objectives:
• To understand a range of texts about a challenging subject area

Learning outcomes:
• To interpret information in a graph and table about spending on fashion
• To write a diary revealing the life of a factory worker in a developing country

Framework objectives:
  R6 Active reading
  R8 Infer and deduce
  Wr19 Reflective writing
  S&L12 Exploratory talk

Introduction

Ask students to turn to pages 88 and 89 in the Students' Book. Use the Introduction and Shared text to focus them on the unit topic. Ask them to find the spread about 'Fashion victims' in the Contents list. Focus on the English skills they will be using. You may wish to give students the self-assessment sheet (**RS A**), to fill in the learning objectives and outcomes.

Starter idea

Ask students to brainstorm words about fashion, e.g. catwalks, models, expensive, fun. Estimate the proportions of positive and negative words. Record the answers, to compare with the same process that will be repeated at the end of the lesson.

Lesson development

• **Introduction** Read the introductory text and check students understand the usual interpretation of the phrase *fashion victim*: someone who follows every fashion trend. *Are there any fashion victims in class? How much do they know about current trends? What are the popular brands? How much do some items cost?*
• **True/False** Ensure that students understand the table and the graph, e.g. how the total on the table is the sum of the other figures. Ask students to work out the True and False questions: 1) False, 2) True.

• **Do you know a fashion victim?** Ask students to interview each other about fashion. **RS 7.4** has suggested questions. There are five closed questions (for easy collation of results) plus space for students to create another question. Explain that it must be a closed question, requiring a yes/no answer.
• **Mara's story** Point out that there are other fashion victims: those people working in the clothing factories in developing countries such as India, China and East Asia. Read the outline of Mara's day and consider the quality of Mara's life. For example,
  – How much does Mara earn for each pair of trousers? (0.6p)
  – If she has a 30 minute lunch break, but no other breaks, how much could Mara earn in a day? (£6)
  – How does this compare with what teenagers spend on fashion?
• Ask students to write Mara's diary, describing the events of her day, her feelings and reactions too. This could be taught as a guided writing session (see below).
• **Plenary** Repeat the brainstorm from the start of the lesson. Have the students' views changed in any way? Who do they think are the real victims of fashion?

Extension idea

Find out more about how the fashion industry affects people like Mara in **RS 7.6**.

Guided writing

This sequence may be helpful:
• Review the task.
• Recap on the information.
• Review the requirements of the text - giving both events and feelings/reactions.
• Draft initial sentence(s) with support.
• Allow time for individual writing.
See **RSs G** and **H** for notes and planning for guided work.

Teaching support

Support could be directed at:
• leading a guided group
• recording the brainstorming in the starter and plenary.

Assessment

Encourage the students to complete the self-assessment sheet, **RS A**. In addition, **RSs B** and **C** can be used for peer and teacher assessment of learning.

7 Fashion

Wild designer

Text type: Instructions, Notes, Plans
Cross-curricular links: Design and Technology, Art

Assessment focuses:
Reading
  AF2 Understand, describe, select or retrieve information, events or ideas from texts
Writing
  AF1 Write imaginative, interesting and thoughtful text
  AF3 Organize and present whole texts effectively, sequencing and structuring information, ideas and events

Learning objectives:
• To plan, research, draft and present a complete project, based on fashion design

Learning outcomes:
• To plan and draft designs for a new fashion accessory
• To produce neat designs and present these to others

Framework objectives:
  R4 Note-making
  Wr1 Drafting process
  Wr10 Organize texts appropriately
  S&L3 Shape a presentation

Introduction

Ask students to turn to pages 88 and 89 in the Students' Book. Use the Introduction and Shared text to focus them on the unit topic. Ask them to find the spread about 'Wild designer' in the Contents list. Focus on the English skills they will be using. You may wish to give students the self-assessment sheet (**RS A**), to fill in the learning objectives and outcomes.

Starter idea

Give students the steps (see below) to create their own design presentation, but jumble them up. Ask students to put them in a logical order.
• Choose the accessory and wildlife theme.
• Research and make notes.
• Plan the overall design.
• Present the design neatly on paper.
• Present the paper designs to an audience.

Lesson development

• **Introduction** Read through the whole spread, so that students have the 'big picture'. Give them the timescale for the project, including the limits for each stage (according to the time you have available).
• Q1 and 2 – At this stage, when students are brainstorming ideas for their projects, it would be helpful to have some example accessories, as well as examples of how wildlife themes are used in fashion.

• Q3 – Encourage students to experiment with patterns, colours and shapes (have coloured pencils available). Ensure that they make notes on the effects they have observed and are trying to create.
• Q4 and 5 – Students should now plan their accessory and ways to present their plans. Give them clear deadlines for completing different parts of their work, e.g. headings, designs, labels. Emphasize the need to explain their choices.
• Q6 – Give students time to prepare their presentations. **RS 7.5** will help them to organize their thoughts and talk.
• It will raise the status of the activity if you can invite an 'expert' to the see the presentations (e.g. an art or D&T teacher, student from design college, jewellery designer).
• **Plenary** If you have been able to invite an expert, ask them for feedback on some of the strengths they have observed in the students' work. Alternatively, ask students to comment on what has impressed them.

Extension ideas

• Organize a cross-curricular visit to a local museum or gallery to study and make notes on design.
• Ask students to research into the background of their chosen accessory. The Victoria and Albert Museum website is a good source www.vam.ac.uk/collections/fashion.

Teaching support

Support could be directed at:
• assisting individuals with their designs
• giving students a dummy run-through with their presentations
• videoing the presentations for future review
• creating a display of the designs.

Assessment

Encourage the students to complete the self-assessment sheet, **RS A**. In addition, **RSs B** and **C** can be used for peer and teacher assessment of learning.

44

7 Fashion

Fashion challenge

Introduction

This final section is designed to test word and sentence level skills. It gives students the opportunity to complete short tasks independently.

The skills are linked to other parts of the unit but the activities stand alone. Students do not need to look back at the rest of the unit, although you may wish to draw their attention to the links as you review their work.

There are two suggested approaches:
1. Students start at number 1 and are allowed to work their way though the activities at their own pace. There are extension ideas for some of the activities for those students who may require them.
2. Allow students time to complete one activity and review it together before moving on to the next task. This may be more supportive to those students who have difficulty working independently.

Task 1

Focus: homophones

The homophones in the list are given below with meanings (although some words have multiple meanings).

blue (colour)/blew (past tense of blow)
waist (middle of body)/waste (unwanted things)
write (put words on paper)/right (correct)
sun (a star)/son (male child)
here (this place)/hear (listen)
dear (much loved)/deer (animal)

Extension: Think up three other pairs of homophones.

Task 2

Focus: open and closed questions

Here are possible responses:

1. Jeans
Closed: *What is the usual colour of jeans?*
Open: *Why are jeans so popular?*

2. hairstyles
Closed: *What is the most popular hairstyle?*
Open: *What does your hairstyle say about you?*

3. a fashion designer
Closed: *How long does it take to train as a fashion designer?*
Open: *Is it a rewarding job?*

Task 3

Focus: quotations

Here are the shortened and sharpened quotations:
- *'Fashion makes us all the same.'*
- *'Colour is everything in fashion.'*
- *'Fashion rules the lives of everyone.'*

Extension: Find some words in this unit which would make a good quotation about fashion. Write them down – remembering to use quotation marks.

Task 4

Focus: opinions

The opinions in the passage are here underlined.

Josh Jolly is <u>a fantastic designer</u>. He has worked in London, Paris and Stoke. This was his third fashion show, and <u>the best so far</u>.

All his dresses were about bubbles. The bubble-wrap dress <u>was stunning</u>. The model had a big shiny bubble hat on – <u>a very clever idea</u>.

However, <u>the best dress was the bubble-gum ball gown</u>. It was in a <u>pretty pink</u> shade. The skirt blew big pink bubbles as the model walked down the catwalk. <u>It was bubble magic!</u>

Teaching support

Support could be directed at:
- helping students to read the instructions
- giving examples and prompts
- monitoring if any students have difficulty with particular skills so that this can be addressed in future lessons
- looking out for students who should be going on to the extension ideas.

Assessment

RS D can be used for self- and teacher assessment of the work done on the unit challenge spreads.

Extended text

There is an extended text, linked to the unit topic on **RS 7.6**. This can be used in a variety of ways to extend the students' skills and to engage them further.

8 Fantasy worlds

Imaginary worlds

Text type: Fiction

Assessment focuses:
Reading
    AF2 Understand, describe, select or retrieve information,
    events or ideas from texts
    AF6 Identify and comment on writers' purposes and
    viewpoints and the overall effect of the texts on the reader

Learning objectives:
• To understand the ingredients of a fantasy story

Learning outcomes:
• To work out a puzzle, giving the typical features of a
  fantasy story
• To use talk and drama to develop a fantasy storyline

Framework objectives:
R12 Character, setting and mood
Wr9 Link writing and reading
S&L12 Exploratory talk
S&L15 Explore in role

Introduction

Ask students to turn to pages 102 and 103 in the Students' Book. Use the Introduction and Shared text to focus them on the unit topic. Ask them to find the spread about 'Imaginary worlds' in the Contents list. Focus on the English skills they will be using. You may wish to give students the self-assessment sheet (**RS A**), to fill in the learning objectives and outcomes.

Starter idea

Play 'Just a Minute'. Ask students to imagine another world – perhaps their ideal world or one from a story they know (e.g. historic, futuristic, magical). Give them each one minute to talk about their world with their partners.

Then, in the style of the Radio 4 programme, ask volunteers to talk about their world for a minute (or 30 seconds) without repetition or hesitation. Comment on what sort of worlds they describe.

Lesson development

• **Introduction** Read the introductory text, perhaps inviting examples of some of the well-known fantasy stories the students have read or seen, e.g. *The Lion, the Witch and the Wardrobe*, *The Lord of the Rings* and *Harry Potter*.

• Q1 – The answers are:
  - *magic*
  - *new places*
  - *evil*
  - *a quest*
  - *creatures*
  - *danger*
  - *strange people.*
  Again, relate these features to stories the students may know.

• **The fantasy story** Read the extract and ensure it is understood before moving on to the activities.

• Organize students into small groups. Encourage them to discuss the first three activities on page 105, before moving on to their improvisation. Draw their attention to the Help box. They will also need to consider other characters who may appear.

• **RS 8.1** can be used for the group to record their discussion and plan their ideas. This can be used as evidence that they are ready (or not) to move on to the next stage – the improvisation.

• Emphasize that the students need only work out the next stage of the story. They do not need to think of the whole story. They will need to decide on how to finish their improvisation, so that it doesn't drift on or fizzle out.

• Ask students to present their ideas.

• **Plenary** 'Hot seat' the main character, asking how he or she knows that they are in a fantasy story. What ingredients have they noticed? Did he or she manage to maintain the fantasy genre?

Extension ideas

• Introduce a prop that must be used in the improvisation, e.g. a key, a hat, a shell.

• Write the next paragraph of the story. It should follow on from the one in the Students' Book.

Teaching support

Support could be directed at:
• being the timer/referee for 'Just a Minute'
• assisting and prompting student discussion activities
• prompting the students to makes notes on their ideas
• making a video or audio recording of the improvisations, so that the strengths and development points can be reviewed.

Assessment

Encourage the students to complete the self-assessment sheet, **RS A**. In addition, **RSs B** and **C** can be used for peer and teacher assessment of learning.

8 Fantasy worlds

Characters

Text type: Fiction

Assessment focuses:
Reading
　AF2 Understand, describe, select or retrieve information,
　events or ideas from texts
　AF3 Deduce, infer or interpret information, events or
　ideas from texts
Writing
　AF1 Write imaginative, interesting and thoughtful texts
　AF3 Organize and present whole texts effectively,
　sequencing and structuring information, ideas and events

Learning objectives:
• To be aware of the types of character in a fantasy story

Learning outcomes:
• To match a list of character types to descriptions
• To create three new game card characters

Framework objectives:
　R1 Locate information
　R12 Character, setting and mood
　Wr6 Characterization
　Wr10 Organize texts appropriately

Introduction

Ask students to turn to pages 102 and 103 in the Students' Book. Use the Introduction and Shared text to focus them on the unit topic. Ask them to find the spread about 'Characters' in the Contents list. Focus on the English skills they will be using. You may wish to give students the self-assessment sheet (**RS A**), to fill in the learning objectives and outcomes.

Starter idea

Play 'Who am I?'. Put a sticky note on the forehead of each student. Each note has a fantasy story character type written on it (e.g. wizard, fairy, elf). The student cannot see the character type, but must try to find it out by asking questions of a partner. The partner can only answer yes or no.

Lesson development

• **Introduction** Read the introductory text, relating the characters to stories that the students know, e.g. Harry Potter is a hero. He has strong magical abilities.
• Q1 – The characters and descriptions should be matched as follows:
  giant – a creature like a huge man
  wizard – a man who uses magic
  knight – a fighter, who has a horse and armour
  witch – a woman who uses magic
  fairy – a small being with magical powers
  alien – a being from another planet or world

• Q2 – Here students must recall three fantasy stories they know. Fantasy stories pervade young people's culture, so even if they haven't read the book they may have seen the film or played the computer game. Many computer games involve magic, quests and strange creatures.
• Q3 – Ask students to identify some types of character in the stories they have identified.
• **Game cards** Draw attention to the examples of game cards on page 107. Game cards give details of a character's attributes, and therefore help to define a character and break him/her down. Ask students to study the features of these characters. What other qualities can they think of which help to define a character, e.g. popularity, resourcefulness, leadership ability.
• Q4 and 5 – ask students to create and name three characters for a fantasy story. They should then design a game card for each character. **RS 8.2** provides a template design, with space for the name, a picture, up to eight qualities and a mark for each quality.
• **Plenary** Ask students to introduce one of their characters to the rest of the class. They should explain how they have defined the character and the choices that they have made.

Extension ideas

• Create further game cards and practise using them.
• Write the rules to the game.

Teaching support

Support could be directed at:
• giving out the sticky notes for the starter activity
• assisting students with the reading and writing tasks
• creating a display of the cards, annotated with features of the characters of fantasy stories.

Assessment

Encourage the students to complete the self-assessment sheet, **RS A**. In addition, **RSs B** and **C** can be used for peer and teacher assessment of learning.

Setting

Text type: Fiction

Assessment focuses:

Reading

AF3 Deduce, infer or interpret information, events or ideas from texts

AF5 Explain and comment on writers' use of language, including grammatical and literary features at word and sentence level

Writing

AF1 Write imaginative, interesting and thoughtful texts

AF7 Select appropriate and effective vocabulary

Learning objectives:
* To be aware of how setting is used in stories

Learning outcomes:
* To explore how the home of a hobbit is described
* To describe the setting at the start of a story

Framework objectives:

R12 Character, setting and mood

R14 Language choices

Wr14 Evocative description

S&L12 Exploratory talk

Introduction

Ask students to turn to pages 102 and 103 in the Students' Book. Use the Introduction and Shared text to focus them on the unit topic. Ask them to find the spread about 'Setting' in the Contents list. Focus on the English skills they will be using. You may wish to give students the self-assessment sheet (**RS A**), to fill in the learning objectives and outcomes.

Starter idea

Play 'Step into the picture'. Provide students with a picture or a photograph showing a setting. (Choose one of the photographs on page 109 if no other pictures are available.) Ask them to imagine they can step into the picture, to pick a place to stand, then look around and describe what they can see. Ask individuals to describe what they can see, hear, smell etc.

Lesson development

* **Introduction** Read the introductory text, and ensure students are clear about what is meant by 'setting'.
* Q1 – Ask students to complete the description of the hobbit's home. The words should be completed in this order: *hole, dirty, worms, round, shiny.*
* Q2 and 3 – Give students time to talk about what the passage tells us and what it implies. Draw attention to the Help box to support their thinking.

* You may wish students to text mark the description of the hobbit's home they have written, circling actual information and annotating what they can infer.
* Q4 – Give students time to study and talk about the pictures, the setting depicted and the type of story to which it might be suited. Encourage them to explain their choices and ideas.
* Q5 – Students should choose one picture and use it as the basis for the setting of a fantasy story. **RS 8.3** gives them a checklist of supportive ideas for their writing. This part of the lesson might be taught as a guided writing session (see below).
* **Plenary** Read and share some of the writing the students have completed, commenting on the techniques they have used to develop setting.

Extension idea

Use **RS 8.6** to find out more about the author of the classic story *The Hobbit*. Look for clues about what influenced Tolkien in his writing.

Guided writing

This sequence may be helpful:
* Review the task.
* Recap on the techniques they might use.
* Review the purpose of the writing: to entertain the reader.
* Model and practise using certain techniques, e.g. describing a detail of one of the pictures.
* Draft initial sentence(s) with support.
* Allow time for individual writing.

See **RSs G** and **H** for notes and planning for guided work.

Teaching support

Support could be directed at:
* leading a guided writing group
* looking out for good examples to be shared in the plenary.

Assessment

Encourage the students to complete the self-assessment sheet, **RS A**. In addition, **RSs B** and **C** can be used for peer and teacher assessment of learning.

8 Fantasy worlds

The story

Introduction

Ask students to turn to pages 102 and 103 in the
Students' Book. Use the Introduction and Shared text
to focus them on the unit topic. Ask them to find the
spread about 'The story' in the Contents list. Focus
on the English skills they will be using. You may wish
to give students the self-assessment sheet (**RS A**), to
fill in the learning objectives and outcomes.

Starter idea

Play 'Add a word'. The class tell a story, but with
each student contributing one word at a time to the
story. For example:
1st student: *Lucy*
2nd student: *hated*
3rd student: *spiders*
4th student: *so*
5th student: *much*
6th student: *that…*
End the game at an appropriate time, e.g. when it
fizzles out or becomes too silly.

Lesson development

• **Introduction** Read the introductory text and
  look carefully at the story structure diagram.
  Explain that, unlike the rambling story they told
  as a starter, successful stories have structure.
• Q1, 2 and 3 – Give pairs time to talk about these
  questions. Draw out the following:
  – *The climax is the most exciting part, e.g. because
  the hero is in terrible danger*

– *The development is the longest part, as the story
  builds and we get to know the characters*
– *It is particularly important for the writer to catch
  the reader's interest at the start of the story, to
  make them want to read on further.*

• Q4 – Use this activity to apply the students'
  knowledge of story structure. Ask them to copy
  out the table, or to use **RS 8.4**, and to complete
  the table for a story they know. This can be a
  traditional story, e.g. *Red Riding Hood*, or a more
  recent story.
• **Dialogue and narrative** Read texts A and B and
  either as a class, or in pairs, complete Q5. Draw
  out how text B has a balance of dialogue and
  narrative and gives more details and insight, etc.
• Q6 – Ask students to write the next part of the
  story, using a mix of narrative and dialogue. Draw
  attention to the Help box. This session may be
  taught at a guided writing session (see below).
• **Plenary** Read and share some of the writing
  they have completed, commenting on the use of
  narrative and dialogue.

Extension idea

Use a comic book extract and ask students to turn it
into a story, with both dialogue and narrative.

Guided writing

This sequence may be helpful:
• Review the task.
• Recap on the techniques they might use:
  narrative and dialogue.
• Model and practise certain skills, e.g. speech
  punctuation.
• Draft initial sentence(s) with support.
• Allow time for individual writing.
See **RSs G** and **H** for notes and planning for
guided work.

Teaching support

Support could be directed at:
• leading a guided writing group
• looking out for good examples to be shared in
  the plenary.

Assessment

Encourage the students to complete the self-assessment
sheet, **RS A**. In addition, **RSs B** and **C** can be used
for peer and teacher assessment of learning.

8 Fantasy worlds

The quest

Text type: Fiction

Assessment focuses:

Reading

    AF4 Identify and comment on the structure and organization of texts

Writing

    AF1 Write imaginative, interesting and thoughtful texts

    AF3 Organize and present whole texts effectively, sequencing and structuring information, ideas and events

    AF7 Select appropriate and effective vocabulary

Learning objectives:

• To plan an extended piece of story writing

Learning outcomes:

• To create a plan for a quest story

Framework objectives:

    Wr5 Story structure

    Wr6 Characterization

    Wr9 Link writing and reading

Introduction

Ask students to turn to pages 102 and 103 in the Students' Book. Use the Introduction and Shared text to focus them on the unit topic. Ask them to find the spread about 'The quest' in the Contents list. Focus on the English skills they will be using. You may wish to give students the self-assessment sheet (**RS A**), to fill in the learning objectives and outcomes.

Starter idea

Play 'Hangman', using some of the vocabulary and skills that have been featured in this unit so far, e.g. character, dialogue, setting. Students play and win in the usual way, by guessing letters and eventually the word. But in order to win properly, they must explain the relevance of the word to story writing. (You might allow them to look back at the unit for help.)

Lesson development

- **Introduction** Read the introductory text and explain the task. Make it clear that the task is to *plan* a story, as opposed to writing the whole story.
- Read through all of the activities to begin with so that students gain the 'big picture'. Explain that they must make choices for most of the tasks.
- **Planning the quest** The activity may be taught as a guided writing session (see below). **RS 8.5** can be used to help students structure their notes. It may be helpful to enlarge this to A3 size for some students.

- If students have difficulty planning tasks, allow them to work with a partner on the first activities, and then work individually on the remainder of the tasks. Encourage them to look back at other parts of this unit that they have studied for support and ideas.
- Give students clear timeframes for each part of the plan.
- **Plenary** Put students in pairs to share their plans. They each have to report back to the rest of the class on one effective aspect of their partner's plan.
- Ask students to write a sentence about how planning can help create an effective story.

Extension idea

Ask students to write out various sections of their story, e.g. the opening, the climax, the last paragraph.

Guided writing

This sequence may be helpful:
- Review the task.
- Recap on the techniques they might use: effective description.
- Model and practise certain skills, e.g. translating their ideas into notes.
- Do the first two or three tasks with a partner.
- Allow time for individual planning.
- Regularly review progress.

See **RSs G** and **H** for notes and planning for guided work.

Teaching support

Support could be directed at:
- leading a guided writing group
- looking out for good examples to be shared in the plenary.

Assessment

Encourage the students to complete the self-assessment sheet, **RS A**. In addition, **RSs B** and **C** can be used for peer and teacher assessment of learning.

8 Fantasy worlds

Fantasy worlds challenge

Introduction

This final section is designed to test word and sentence level skills. It gives students the opportunity to complete short tasks independently.

The skills are linked to other parts of the unit but the activities stand alone. Students do not need to look back at the rest of the unit, although you may wish to draw their attention to the links as you review their work.

There are two suggested approaches:
1. Students start at number 1 and are allowed to work their way though the activities at their own pace. There are extension ideas for some of the activities for those students who may require them.
2. Allow students time to complete one activity and review it together before moving on to the next task. This may be more supportive to those students who have difficulty working independently.

Task 1

Focus: spelling

Here is a selection of words students might find in the word 'fantasy'.

an	as	at	*fan*	*fat*	*sty*	*ant*
ants	*any*	*nay*	*tan*	*tans*	*aft*	*fast*
stay	*sat*	*say*	*nasty*			

Task 2

Focus: speech marks

Here is the passage with the speech marks restored:

> "Hi," said Joe. The girl did not say anything.
> "I'm Joe. What's your name?" asked Joe.
> "Steffi," she said.
> "Nice to meet you, Steffi."

Extension: Continue the conversation, punctuating the speech correctly.

Task 3

Focus: tenses

Here is the passage with the verbs in present tense changed to past tense:

> Steffi <u>looked</u> around. Water ran down the slimy walls. Cobwebs <u>blew</u> about in the empty windows. Then she saw a pair of eyes glowing in the shadows. They <u>were</u> like nothing she <u>had</u> ever seen. She <u>shivered</u>.

Extension: Continue the story for three sentences, ensuring it remains in past tense.

Task 4

Focus: story structure

Here are the story stages matched with the descriptions.

Introduction	Joe buys an odd red candle from a junk shop.
Development	When the candle is lit, it takes him to a land ruled by the evil witch, Morda. He meets Steffi. Her father has been taken to the witch's cliff top castle. They go to free him.
Climax	Morda finds out and traps Joe. The candle will give her extra powers. Trying to kill Joe, she slips and falls to her death.
Ending	Joe and Steffi find her father and return home happy. Joe has to return to his own world.

Extension: Choose one of the stages and write a short paragraph of the story.

Teaching support

Support could be directed at:
*   helping students to read the instructions
*   giving examples and prompts
*   monitoring if any students have difficulty with particular skills so that this can be addressed in future lessons
*   looking out for students who should be going on to the extension ideas.

Assessment

RS D can be used for self- and teacher assessment of the work done on the unit challenge spreads.

Extended text

There is an extended text, linked to the unit topic on **RS 8.6**. This can be used in a variety of ways to extend the students' skills and to engage them further.

9 Funny ha ha

Having a laugh

> **Text type:** Information, Description
>
> **Assessment focuses:**
> Reading
>   AF2 Understand, describe, select or retrieve information,
>   events or ideas from texts
>   AF5 Explain and comment on writers' use of language
> Writing
>   AF1 Write imaginative, interesting and thoughtful texts
>   AF7 select appropriate and effective vocabulary
>
> **Learning objectives:**
> • To use reading and talk to explore what makes us laugh
>
> **Learning outcomes:**
> • To read and complete a text about laughter
> • To describe how people look and sound when they laugh
>
> **Framework objectives:**
>   R2 Extract information
>   Wr14 Evocative description
>   S&L6 Recall main points
>   S&L12 Exploratory talk

Introduction

Ask students to turn to pages 116 and 117 in the Students' Book. Use the Introduction and Shared text to focus them on the unit topic. Ask them to find the spread about 'Having a laugh' in the Contents list. Focus on the English skills they will be using. You may wish to give students the self-assessment sheet (**RS A**), to fill in the learning objectives and outcomes.

Starter idea

Play 'Laughter synonyms'. First, challenge your students to think up as many synonyms for 'laugh' as they can in one minute, e.g. *chuckle, giggle, snigger, smile, grin.* Next, ask them to perform one type of laugh (e.g. chuckle), for others to guess the synonym. The idea is to look for the subtleties of interpretation that synonyms can bring.

Lesson development

- **Introduction** Read the introductory text and ask students for further ideas about what makes us laugh, e.g. funny adverts, cartoons, comedy programmes.
- Read through the cloze passage and ask students to fill in the blanks using the suggestions given.
- Q1 – In pairs, students should discuss what makes them laugh. Draw attention to the Help box and encourage them to give examples. Promote close listening skills by asking students to report back on what their partner finds funny.

- **Types of Laughter** Laughter is quite a complex activity (remind them of the synonyms). Explain how similes can create a better image of laughter. Read the examples given.
- Q2 – Writing a description of someone they know well, is more likely to produce something original as opposed to a clichéd description.
- Ask students to focus on the *sound* of the laughter. Suggest that they close their eyes to remember the sound, or to listen to the laughter of a friend. **RS 9.1** provides an example, as well as space for notes and the description.
- Q3 – The emphasis here is looking at detail and avoiding clichéd ideas. You may want to provide photographs of people laughing.
- Q4 – The animal traditionally associated with laughing is the hyena, although they are not traditionally perceived in a good light (e.g. they are scavengers, and think of their portrayal in *The Lion King*). Discuss whether this shows another side of laughter.
- **Plenary** Ask students to finish this sentence: *Having a good laugh means…* They can use any of the ideas they have explored during the lesson.

Extension idea

Use the extension text on **RS 9.6** to look at how similes can be used effectively in stories. It describes a character from a story called *The Thief of Always* by Clive Barker. Ask students to explore what the description tells them about the character.

Teaching support

Support could be directed at:
- noting students' ideas during the starter
- assisting the other activities by providing models, questions and ideas
- researching pictures of people laughing for Q3.

Assessment

Encourage the students to complete the self-assessment sheet, **RS A**. In addition, **RSs B** and **C** can be used for peer and teacher assessment of learning.

9 Funny ha ha

Funny people

Text type: Instructions, Poetry
Cross-curricular links: Art, Design

Assessment focuses:
Writing
  AF1 Write imaginative, interesting and thoughtful texts
  AF3 Organize and present whole texts effectively,
  sequencing and structuring information, ideas and events

Learning objectives:
* To create effective instructions
* To write an acrostic poem

Learning outcomes:
* To instruct another student on how to complete a design
* To compose an acrostic poem called 'clown'.

Framework objectives:
  S13d Instructions
  Wr8 Visual and sound effects
  Wr13 Instructions and directions
  S&L4 Answers, instructions, explanations

Introduction

Ask students to turn to pages 116 and 117 in the Students' Book. Use the Introduction and Shared text to focus them on the unit topic. Ask them to find the spread about 'Funny people' in the Contents list. Focus on the English skills they will be using. You may wish to give students the self-assessment sheet (**RS A**), to fill in the learning objectives and outcomes.

Starter idea

Play 'Acrostics'. Think of a word and then give the students a series of word clues. The first letter of each word will spell out the original word. For example:
Word = FROG
   Word clues:
   A number after four **F**ive
   This light stops cars **R**ed
   The opposite of young **O**ld
   A small green or red fruit **G**rape

Lesson development

* **Introduction** Read the introductory text and ask students for further ideas about who makes them laugh.
* Q1 – The red nose is a familiar prop used by clowns and has become symbolic of comedy. Students can pick out other features of clowns, hidden in the ring of words. The words are: *red nose, wig, big feet, bright clothes, make up, hat.*
* **Clown faces** Various traditions have grown up around clowns. One of them is for working clowns to have their face design recorded on an egg. Draw students' attention to the pictures of eggs on the page.

* Q2, 3 and 4 – Ask students to create their own simple clown face design. Emphasize the need for simplicity, and give a strict time limit for creating the designs. Advise students to keep their designs out of sight of others.
* Once the designs are complete, students should pair up, ideally sitting back-to-back. Each student must instruct the other on how to draw the design they have created, without showing them the picture.
* The success of the verbal instructions should be evident by comparing the pictures. If you have time, ask them to jointly write clear instructions for creating one of the designs. Encourage them to use terms such as *first, then, next, finally.*
* Q5 – Ask students to write an acrostic poem using the word 'clown'. This could be taught as a guided writing session (see below). Emphasize that their poem should be more developed than the puzzles they looked at for the starter.
* **RS 9.2** provides support and a template for the acrostic poem. Model writing one, perhaps using this example:
  Crazy and daft, clowns show off with
  Loud actions, falling
  Over and over and over.
  With giant flapping shoes and big red
  Noses, unmissable.
* **Plenary** Share and enjoy some of the acrostics that the students have written.

Extension idea

Students can choose a funny person that they like and write an acrostic about them.

Guided writing

This sequence may be helpful:
* Review the task.
* Review the requirements of the text.
* Model writing the first line.
* Allow time for individual writing.
* Review their progress.
See **RSs G** and **H** for notes and planning for guided work.

Teaching support

Support could be directed at:
* creating words and clues for the starter
* leading a guided group.

Assessment

Encourage the students to complete the self-assessment sheet, **RS A**. In addition, **RSs B** and **C** can be used for peer and teacher assessment of learning.

Funny rhymes

Text type: Poetry

Assessment focuses:
Reading
AF5 Explain and comment on writers' use of language, including grammatical and literary features at work and sentence level
AF6 Identify and comment on writers' purposes and viewpoints and the overall effect of the text on the reader

Learning objectives:
• To investigate humour in poetry

Learning outcomes:
• To study three poems and analyse the features that make them funny

Framework objectives:
R14 Language choices
R19 Poetic form
S&L12 Exploratory talk
S&L13 Collaboration

Introduction

Ask students to turn to pages 116 and 117 in the Students' Book. Use the Introduction and Shared text to focus them on the unit topic. Ask them to find the spread about 'Funny rhymes' in the Contents list. Focus on the English skills they will be using. You may wish to give students the self-assessment sheet (**RS A**), to fill in the learning objectives and outcomes.

Starter idea

Focus on one of the features they will be looking at during the lesson by playing the 'Rhyming game'.

Have a list of words, each of which has a string of common rhyming words, e.g. gate, cat, fight. Select one in your mind, and challenge students to find out the chosen word. Give them a clue by saying one word which rhymes with it. Go around the class and give students, one at a time, an opportunity to guess the word. However, they should not say the actual word, but instead should give a definition. For example:

The chosen word = 'gate'
Tell the class it rhymes with 'mate'.
Student 1: *Is it something you eat dinner off?*
Teacher: *No, it's not 'plate'.*
Student 2: *Is it the opposite of love?*
Teacher: *No, it's not 'hate'.*
Student 3: *Is it a door in a garden?*
Teacher: *Yes, it's 'gate'.*

Lesson development

• **Introduction** Read the three poems and check the students' understanding. Have they read any of them before, or anything like them? Do they recognize the limerick form? Do they know any other limericks?

• **Poetry explorer** This provides a framework for students to explore and talk about the poems. It is designed to help students engage with the poems and form a personal response to them. It looks at aspects of structure and language, and how these contribute to a humorous text.

• Read through the poetry explorer, and ensure that students can see the possible routes through it.

• Put students into pairs and ask them to choose a poem to explore. They should trace their way through the poetry explorer answering every question in turn.

• **RS 9.3** provides a framework for students to make notes as they go through the explorer.

• **Plenary** Ask students to finish this statement: *Some things that make this poem funny are...* They can do this either as a class or in pairs, presenting their ideas to another pair.

Extension ideas

• Write a paragraph about what makes the poem funny.

• Research other humorous poems, and investigate them using the poetry explorer.

• Write their own humorous poem, in the style of the one they have explored.

• Challenge students to learn and recite their favourite humorous poem

Teaching support

Support could be directed at:
• prompting students with definitions for the starter
• assisting students as they explore their chosen poems
• helping with extension tasks, e.g. researching poetry anthologies that include suitable humorous poems.

Assessment

Encourage the students to complete the self-assessment sheet, **RS A**. In addition, **RSs B** and **C** can be used for peer and teacher assessment of learning.

9 Funny ha ha

Funny creatures

Introduction

Ask students to turn to pages 116 and 117 in the Students' Book. Use the Introduction and Shared text to focus them on the unit topic. Ask them to find the spread about 'Funny creatures' in the Contents list. Focus on the English skills they will be using. You may wish to give students the self-assessment sheet (**RS A**), to fill in the learning objectives and outcomes.

Starter idea

Practise performance skills and build confidence in speaking in front of others by playing 'Say it in five'. Give pairs or small groups of students a word, e.g. 'chocolate', and challenge them to say it in five different ways. Model some ideas, e.g:
• outraged
• questioning
• whispering
• hissing
• confidentially.
Reward/praise original approaches.
Alternatively, instruct students to say it in one way and other students must guess the instruction.

Lesson development

• **Introduction** Read the poem, 'Phinniphin', with the class, preferably more than once. For example, read around the class, a student taking a line at a time. Discuss what is happening, where it is set, what they think the Phinniphin are, etc.
• Q1 – Ask pairs or small groups to prepare a reading of the poem. Emphasize that the reading is to entertain an audience and suggest ways of delivering it, e.g. choral reading, one person reading while others mime suitable actions, different people reading different parts. Make suggestions for actions (e.g. hand actions, use of eyes/head/body) and sound effects (e.g. waves, wind).
• Q2 – Allow enough time and space for the performances and give positive and constructive feedback. If possible, video the performances so that the students themselves can evaluate them better.
• Q3 – Ask them to create an information page on Phinniphin. They will need to break the subject down into areas, e.g. appearance, habits, where they live, diet, likes and dislikes, and consider how to present the information, e.g. text, pictures, diagrams.
• Refer them to the Help box for support. **RS 9.4** has a framework to support their planning and writing. (You may wish to enlarge this to A3.) This session could be taught as a guided writing session (see below).
• **Plenary** Ask students to create:
   – one golden rule for giving a group performance (e.g. listen carefully to the ideas of others)
   – one golden rule to writing an information text (e.g. plan your work first).

Extension idea

Ask students to make up their own imaginary creature, and to write a poem or an information text about it.

Guided writing

This sequence may be helpful:
• Review the task.
• Review the requirements of the text.
• Model writing the first line.
• Allow time for individual writing.
• Review their progress.
See **RSs G** and **H** for notes and planning for guided work.

Teaching support

Support could be directed at:
• videoing student performances
• leading a guided group.

Assessment

Encourage the students to complete the self-assessment sheet, **RS A**. In addition, **RSs B** and **C** can be used for peer and teacher assessment of learning.

9 Funny ha ha

Tell us another…

Text type: Jokes, Descriptions

Assessment focuses:

Reading
  AF6 Identify and comment on writers' purposes and
  viewpoints and the overall effect of the text on the reader

Writing
  AF2 Produce texts which are appropriate to tasks, reader
  and purpose
  AF3 Organize and present whole texts effectively,
  sequencing and structuring information, ideas and events

Learning objectives:
• Understand how texts can use ambiguity and puns

Learning outcomes:
• To spot and explain the use of puns in jokes
• To correct ambiguity in a text

Framework objectives:
  S6 Resolve ambiguity
  S16 Speech and writing
  Wr14 Evocative description
  S&L2 Recount

Introduction

Ask students to turn to pages 116 and 117 in the
Students' Book. Use the Introduction and Shared text
to focus them on the unit topic. Ask them to find the
spread entitled 'Tell us another…' in the Contents list.
Focus on the English skills they will be using. You may
wish to give students the self-assessment sheet (**RS A**),
to fill in the learning objectives and outcomes.

Starter idea

Play 'Joke dominoes', using **RS 9.5**. Cut up the
cards so that there is a question on one side of the
domino and an unrelated punchline on the other.
Shuffle, then give out all the cards.

One person reads out the question half. The rest listen
carefully. The person with the punchline, reads it out.
Then he or she reads the question on the other half.
So the game goes on, until all the jokes are told. Tip:
for the dominoes to work, it's important to keep to
the order, so keep a master copy to keep track!

Lesson development

• **Introduction** Read the introductory text and
  the jokes on the page. Have the students heard
  any of them before? Everyone has opinions on
  good and bad jokes, so which one is the best
  joke? Explain that you'll be looking at what
  makes some jokes funny.

• **Puns** Read the information on puns and ensure
  they understand what a pun is. Draw attention to
  how the pun in the 'fun guy' joke is explained.
  Move on to Q1, and see if – in pairs – they can
  explain the meanings of 'date' implied in the
  second pun joke, e.g. the word 'date' can mean to
  go out with someone, and in this joke it can also
  mean the fruit.

• **Q2 and 3** – Encourage students to identify and
  explain the other jokes on the page that use puns
  or near puns, i.e. 'chick to chick' (cheek to
  cheek) and 'Boo who?' (boo hoo).

• **Q4** – can they remember or create a joke using a
  pun? Use some of the examples from **RS 9.5** to
  get them thinking.

• **Q5** – The humour in the insurance claim
  descriptions comes from the ambiguity. Ask
  students to discuss why they are funny. Suggest they
  think about the pictures created in their mind.

• **Q6** – Draw attention to the Help box which
  gives an example of how the description could
  be written more clearly. Ask students to rewrite
  the remaining descriptions so that the ambiguity
  is removed

• **Plenary** Repeat the game of 'Joke dominoes'.
  Are they listening carefully? Can they do it
  quicker this time?

Extension idea

Encourage further exploration into different formats
for jokes (e.g. knock knock; Doctor, doctor;
lightbulb jokes) and how they work.

Teaching support

Support could be directed at:
• keeping track of the order of the 'dominoes' in
  the starter
• assisting with the tasks and extension activities.

Assessment

Encourage the students to complete the self-assessment
sheet, **RS A**. In addition, **RSs B** and **C** can be used
for peer and teacher assessment of learning.

9 Funny ha ha

Funny ha ha challenge

Introduction

This final section is designed to test word and sentence level skills. It gives students the opportunity to complete short tasks independently.

The skills are linked to other parts of the unit but the activities stand alone. Students do not need to look back at the rest of the unit, although you may wish to draw their attention to the links as you review their work.

There are two suggested approaches:
1. Students start at number 1 and are allowed to work their way though the activities at their own pace. There are extension ideas for some of the activities for those students who may require them.
2. Allow students time to complete one activity and review it together before moving on to the next task. This may be more supportive to those students who have difficulty working independently.

Task 1

Focus: punctuation

There is no one right answer, and it is a good opportunity to discuss the reasoning behind the punctuation.
Here are two versions of how the joke might be punctuated.

> Knock, knock.
> Who's there?
> Robin.
> Robin who?
> Robin you, so give us all your money!

> Knock! Knock!
> Who's there?
> Robin.
> Robin who?
> Robin you, so give us all your money!

Task 2

Focus: syllables

The number of syllables is indicated at the end of each line.

There was an old man with a beard	*8*
Who said it is just as I feared	*8*
Two owls and a hen	*5*
Four larks and a wren	*5*
Have all built their nests in my beard.	*8*

Task 3

Focus: nouns and verbs

Q: What is the difference between a tree and a train?
A: One sheds its leaves, and the other leaves its shed.
The other word in the joke which is both a **noun** and a **verb** is *leaves*.

The noun *leaves* = green growths on trees
The verb *leaves* = goes away

Extension: Think up other words that are both a noun and a verb (e.g. whisper, jump, fight, swim, judge, hit, joke).

Task 4

Focus: similes

There are no particular right answers, of course, but here are some suggested similes for comparison.
● *The sea was like a hungry monster.*
● *The puppy was like a bouncy ball.*
● *The lesson was as boring as a brick wall.*

Extension: Create their own original simile about the subject of their choice, e.g. a sport, a television programme, a friend.

Teaching support

Support could be directed at:
● helping students to read the instructions
● giving examples and prompts
● monitoring if any students have difficulty with particular skills so that this can be addressed in future lessons
● looking out for students who should be going on to extension work.

Assessment

RS D can be used for self- and teacher assessment of the work done on the unit challenge spreads.

Extended text

There is an extended text, linked to the unit topic on **RS 9.6**. This can be used in a variety of ways to extend the students' skills and to engage them further.

10 Deserts

Deserts of the world

Text type: Information
Cross-curricular links: Geography

Assessment focuses:
Reading
  AF2 Understand, describe, select or retrieve information, events or ideas from texts
Writing
  AF5 Vary sentences for clarity, purpose and effect
  AF6 Write with technical accuracy of syntax and punctuation in phrases, clauses and sentences

Learning objectives:
• To use reading skills to find information
• To plan and organize research

Learning outcomes:
• To complete a map reading and spelling puzzle on deserts

Framework objectives:
  R2 Extract information
  R6 Active reading
  Wr2 Planning formats

Introduction

Ask students to turn to pages 130 and 131 in the Students' Book. Use the Introduction and Shared text to focus them on the unit topic. Ask them to find the spread about 'Deserts of the world' in the Contents list. Focus on the English skills they will be using. You may wish to give students the self-assessment sheet (**RS A**), to fill in the learning objectives and outcomes.

Starter idea

Play 'Give me five'. Draw out the students' existing knowledge of deserts by giving pairs one minute to write down five things they know about deserts. Share and discuss their answers. Make a note of interesting facts that can be used later in the lesson.

Lesson development

• **Introduction** Read the introductory text and study the map which shows some of the world's deserts. Read out the names. Ask students if they have heard of any of them, and if so, when (possibly in the news, or in geography lessons). Explore what the map tells us about the deserts, e.g. their size, location. Again, you could play 'Give me five' about the information on the map.
• Q1 – Ask students to write out the names as they should be, using capital letters, i.e. Atacama, Namib, Mojave, Sahara, Arabian. Can they see the link between the missing letters, i.e. they are all 'a'?
• Q2 – In order to complete this activity, students will need to read the map. Remind them that when the word 'desert' is used as part of a proper

noun, e.g. Atacama Desert, it needs a capital letter. Encourage variety in their responses. In addition to the example in the Students' Book, suitable responses might be:
– *The Namib Desert is found in Africa.*
– *Mojave is a desert in North America.*
– *Africa is where you will find the Sahara Desert.*
– *The Arabian Desert is an Asian desert.*
• Q3 – Draw attention to the 'Did you know?' facts on the page. Point out how much 250 mm is on a ruler. Very often rainfall in a desert is less than 100 mm per year. In the UK the average rainfall is around 1,000 mm. If possible, refer back to points made in the starter.
• Explain that it's important to plan research. Introduce the KWL grid. Ask students to copy it out or use the grid provided on **RS 10.1**. Model how to complete the grid, e.g. completing the first two columns then researching the answer further on in the unit. For example:

What I already **know**	What **I want** to know	What I have **learned**
The Sahara is the biggest desert in the world.	Does anyone live there?	People do live there. They are mainly nomadic and move from place to place.

Give students time to start filling in the grid. You might suggest a minimum number of questions, e.g. three.
• **Plenary** Each student should report one thing they have learned. (This can be done in pairs, with one student reporting back what their partner now knows.)

Extension idea

Allow time for further research on deserts, encouraging students to ask further questions and seek answers from a variety of sources.

Teaching support

Support could be directed at:
• noting students' ideas during the starter activity
• assisting the other activities with models, questions and ideas
• helping with the extension task.

Assessment

Encourage the students to complete the self-assessment sheet, **RS A**. In addition, **RSs B** and **C** can be used for peer and teacher assessment of learning.

10 Deserts

Sand dunes

Text type: Poetry
Cross-curricular links: Geography

Assessment focuses:
Reading
   AF4 Identify and comment on the structure and organization of texts
Writing
   AF1 Write imaginative, interesting and thoughtful texts
   AF3 Organize and present whole texts effectively, sequencing and structuring information, ideas and events

Learning objectives:
• To understand how poems can be presented imaginatively

Learning outcomes:
• To create a shape poem inspired by sand dunes

Framework objectives:
   R11 Print, sound and image
   R14 Language choices
   Wr8 Visual and sound effects
   S&L1 Clarify through talk

Introduction

Ask students to turn to page 130 and 131 in the Students' Book. Use the Introduction and Shared text to focus them on the unit topic. Ask them to find the spread about 'Sand dunes' in the Contents list. Focus on the English skills they will be using. You may wish to give students the self-assessment sheet (**RS A**), to fill in the learning objectives and outcomes.

Starter idea

(This task is best done before revealing the objectives.)
a) Ask students to guess the missing word (sand) that comes before all these words:
   _____ paper
   _____ castle
   _____ stone.
   Can they think of any other words beginning with the word 'sand'? (e.g. sandbag, sandwich, sand dune)
   Can they explain what a sand dune is?
b) If you have space, put students into groups and ask one to become a sculptor. The sculptor must sculpt the rest of the group into the shape of sand dunes.

Lesson development

• **Introduction** Read the introductory text and give students time to study the pictures of the dunes. Can they describe the shapes? (Look at the glossary for help.) How have the shapes formed? Which one forms the most appealing shape?
• Q1 and 2 – Ask students to look at both of the shape poems in turn. Encourage them to discuss how the shape and in the case of poem 2, the

shape and colour, help and echo the meanings? Which poem do they think is most effective? Why? How else could the same meaning be shown in a shape poem?
• Q3 – Ask students to create their own shape poem about sand dunes. They will need to think of what 'angle' to take, e.g. the huge shapes, the movement, the heat, the wind. Encourage them to consider shape and colour, as well as words. When they have decided on their initial ideas, they should plan and draft their work. This could be a guided writing session (see below).
• **RS 10.2** provides template shapes. Students can use the lines as writing guides or fill the spaces with words.
• Draw attention to the Help box which provides a helpful word bank.
• **Plenary** Present a partner's ideas to the rest of the class, pointing out one or two effective features. Or, ask students to complete this sentence: *Shape poems can be effective because…*

Extension ideas

• Create a shape poem on a subject of their choosing.
• Find examples of shape poems in published anthologies.
• Use ICT to develop their ideas.

Guided writing

This sequence may be helpful:
• Review the task.
• Review the requirements of the text.
• Model writing the drafting words.
• Allow time for individual writing.
• Review their progress and redraft.
See **RSs G** and **H** for notes and planning for guided work.

Teaching support

Support could be directed at:
• modelling how to discuss the shapes of the dunes and the poems
• assisting students' planning, e.g. through scribing initial ideas
• helping students to use and add to the word bank provided
• finding other examples of shape poems to support extension tasks.

Assessment

Encourage the students to complete the self-assessment sheet, **RS A**. In addition, **RSs B** and **C** can be used for peer and teacher assessment of learning.

Sahara

Text type: Information
Cross-curricular links: Geography, Maths

Assessment focuses:
Reading
AF2 Understand, describe, select or retrieve information, events or ideas from texts
Writing
AF5 Vary sentences for clarity, purpose and effect
AF6 Write with technical accuracy of syntax and punctuation in phrases, clauses and sentences

Learning objectives:
• To understand that data and ideas can be presented in different ways
• To use complex sentences

Learning outcomes:
• To find different ways of presenting the same data
• To create a series of complex sentences about the Sahara

Framework objectives:
S1 Subordinate clauses
R2 Extract information
R7 Identify main ideas

Introduction

Ask students to turn to pages 130 and 131 in the Students' Book. Use the Introduction and Shared text to focus them on the unit topic. Ask them to find the spread about the Sahara in the Contents list. Focus on the English skills they will be using. You may wish to give students the self-assessment sheet (**RS A**), to fill in the learning objectives and outcomes.

Starter idea

Play 'The connectives game'. Put students in threes and give them a topic of conversation, e.g. what they had for lunch. Two of them have a timed conversation while the other one is the referee. During the conversation they must not say *and* or *but*. The referee tallies how many times each of them say *and* or *but*. The winner has the least points. The game should encourage the students to use a wider range of connectives.

Lesson development

• **Introduction** Read the introductory text and draw attention to the map. Discuss what the map shows, and what they can tell about the Sahara from the map, e.g. it is in Africa, it covers a large area.

• Q1 and 2 – Put students into pairs and ask them to discuss the answers to these questions. The Sahara covers about a third of Africa. How do they know the other answers are not correct? Can they express a third in another way? (For example, 33%)

• For Q2 you may wish to write one-quarter as a fraction. Draw attention to the Help box. This may help them work out the answer: 25%.

• Discuss which piece of data they find most helpful.

• Q3 – Read the hot facts about the Sahara. Explain how lots of simple sentences can sound like a list of facts. Complex sentences help to move away from this and add variety to writing. Model how to create a complex sentence
    a) by adding a connective, e.g. *The Sahara is very dry **because** it gets less than 8 cm of rain a year.*
    b) by changing the word order, e.g. *Dust storms can blow for days, **leaving everything covered in sand**.*
    Ask students to make each pair of sentences into one complex one. As in the starter activity, dissuade them from using *and* and *but*.

• **RS 10.3** provides students with a framework for their sentences.

• **Plenary** Ask students to think of two different ways in which numerical data can be presented to help the reader understand it (e.g. as a fraction, as a percentage, in a graph).

• Ask students to write a complex sentence describing two things they have learned in this lesson.

Extension idea

Carry out some further research on the Sahara and write two complex sentences to sum up what they have found out.

Teaching support

Support could be directed at:
• assisting discussion of the activities and modelling how to create complex sentences
• suggesting sources to research more information on the Sahara to support the extension tasks.

Assessment

Encourage the students to complete the self-assessment sheet, **RS A**. In addition, **RSs B** and **C** can be used for peer and teacher assessment of learning.

10 Deserts

Survival

Text type: Advice, Questions
Cross-curricular links: Geography

Assessment focuses:
Reading
  AF2 Understand, describe, select or retrieve information,
  events or ideas from texts
Writing
  AF6 Write with technical accuracy of syntax and
  punctuation in phrases, clauses and sentences

Learning objectives:
• To give accurate answers to questions on a text

Learning outcomes:
• To complete a survival quiz
• To create another question about survival

Framework objectives:
  R2 Extract information
  R6 Active reading
  S&L4 Answers, instructions, explanations
  S&L7 Pertinent questions

Introduction

Ask students to turn to pages 130 and 131 in the Students' Book. Use the Introduction and Shared text to focus them on the unit topic. Ask them to find the spread about 'Survival' in the Contents list. Focus on the English skills they will be using. You may wish to give students the self-assessment sheet (**RS A**), to fill in the learning objectives and outcomes.

Starter idea

Play 'The survival game'. Give small groups of students the following list –
• an umbrella
• a book
• a scarf
• a large bottle of water
• a box of matches
• a large bag of crisps
Advise them that they are stranded in the desert. They can take five items with them, but must leave one behind. They should discuss each item and its potential uses, before making their choices. **RS 10.4** has space for students to make notes on their choices, and this may help structure their discussion.

Encourage creativity, e.g. the umbrella can be used for shade, protection from wind, collecting rain water. There are no right or wrong answers (although crisps are not the best food when dehydrated) and it is the discussion that is important. Encourage the students to listen carefully to each other, and to make sure everyone contributes their ideas.

Lesson development

• **Introduction** Read the introductory text and the survival handbook. Ensure that the students understand the point of each bit of advice. Are there any other good survival tips that they can think of?
• Q1 – Direct pairs of students to complete the survival quiz. The answers are all found in the text of *The Survival Handbook*, and are as follows:
  1. water
  2. from the hot sun
  3. sweating
  4. at night
  5. drink 1 litre of water per hour.
• Q2 – Ask them to write their own question about desert survival, e.g. How long does a sand storm last? How long can you last without water? Should you stay put or look for help?
• **Plenary** Share the questions that students have composed. Is there any duplication? Does anyone know any of the answers? Where would the answers be found?
• If using the KWL grid (from Students' Book, p.133 and **RS 10.1**), add the question to the grid.

Extension ideas

• Challenge students to research the answers to the questions they have raised, possibly researching them in pairs.
• Read the extension text **RS 10.6** on how to signal for help. Work out the key messages from the text, e.g. light a fire to get noticed, and arrange the advice in easy-to-read bulleted points.

Teaching support

Support could be directed at:
• assisting the discussion activities, sometimes as a source of ideas ('A scarf would be good for protecting the face') and sometimes as devil's advocate ('You don't need a scarf to keep warm in the desert!')
• helping students to phrase questions
• assisting with the extension tasks.

Assessment

Encourage the students to complete the self-assessment sheet, **RS A**. In addition, **RSs B** and **C** can be used for peer and teacher assessment of learning.

Snakes and spiders

Text type: Information, Poetry
Cross-curricular links: Geography, Biology

Assessment focuses:
Reading
   AF5 Explain and comment on writers' use of language, including grammatical and literacy features at word and sentence level
Writing
   AF1 Write imaginative, interesting and thoughtful texts
   AF7 Select appropriate and effective vocabulary

Learning objectives:
• To explore word choices in poetry

Learning outcomes:
• To understand the effect of words and letters in a poem about a snake
• To write more lines for the poem

Framework objectives:
   R2 Extract information
   R14 Language choices
   Wr8 Visual and sound effects
   Wr9 Link reading and writing

Introduction

Ask students to turn to pages 130 and 131 in the Students' Book. Use the Introduction and Shared text to focus them on the unit topic. Ask them to find the spread about 'Snakes and spiders' in the Contents list. Focus on the English skills they will be using. You may wish to give students the self-assessment sheet (**RS A**), to fill in the learning objectives and outcomes.

Starter idea

Play 'The alliteration game'. This is an alphabet game in which you go around the class and ask students to name an animal and describe it alliteratively, e.g.
Student 1: an argumentative ape
Student 2: a buzzing bee
Student 3: a careless crow.

Lesson development

• **Introduction** Read the introductory text and ask students to work out the name of the spider in the web: a black widow. This spider is found in many of the American deserts. The female often kills and eats the male after mating.
• Q1 - Read the rattlesnake poem. The poem does not have a title. Ask students to discuss what the missing title could be. Encourage them to look carefully at the text and to back up their ideas with reasons.

• Q2 – Focus on the sound of the words used in the poem. **RS 10.5** has the text of the poem and this can be used for highlighting the use of the letter 's' and the alliteration in the poem. Twenty-three words contain an 's' and the following words begin and end in an 's':
   – slits
   – slips
   – stops
   – something's
   – strikes.
Discuss the alliterative effect of the repeated 's' and how it is particularly effective for describing a snake.
• Q3 – Ask students to add some more lines to the poem. Draw their attention to the Help box for ideas. Use **RS 10.5** to continue writing the poem. This part of the lesson could be taught as a guided writing session (see below).
• **Plenary** Share and compare the extra lines for the poem written by the students. They can be read out by the students or the teacher.

Extension ideas

• Write their own poem, in the same concise style, about the black widow spider.
• If using the KWL grid (**RS 10.1**), add questions on wildlife in the desert.

Guided writing

This sequence may be helpful:
• Review the task.
• Review the requirements of the text, using the Help box.
• Model how to put another line together.
• Allow time for individual writing.
• Review their progress and redraft.
See **RSs G** and **H** for notes and planning for guided work.

Teaching support

Support could be directed at:
• prompting students if necessary on the starter task
• leading a guided group
• looking for examples to be read out for the plenary
• assisting with the extension activities.

Assessment

Encourage the students to complete the self-assessment sheet, **RS A**. In addition, **RSs B** and **C** can be used for peer and teacher assessment of learning.

Desert challenge

Introduction

This final section is designed to test word and sentence level skills. It gives students the opportunity to complete short tasks independently.

The skills are linked to other parts of the unit but the activities stand alone. Students do not need to look back at the rest of the unit, although you may wish to draw their attention to the links as you review their work.

There are two suggested approaches:
1. Students start at number 1 and are allowed to work their way though the activities at their own pace. There are extension ideas for some of the activities for those students who may require them.
2. Allow students time to complete one activity and review it together before moving on to the next task. This may be more supportive to those students who have difficulty working independently.

Task 1

Focus: thesaurus skills

The words fit under these headings:
HOT: warm, boiling, scorching, baking, burning, red-hot
COLD: freezing, icy, chilly, cool, sub-zero, bitter

Extension:

- Choose two hot words or cold words and describe the shades of difference in meaning.
- Use a thesaurus to find synonyms for DRY and WET.

Task 2

Focus: hyphens

There are no right answers. Here are some possibilities:
Orange-ginger
Silver-pink
Amber-gold

Extension: Encourage students to create their own colours using a wider range of colours, e.g. purples, blues and blacks, for a night sky.

Task 3

Focus: alliteration

There are no right answers. Here are some possibilities:
- The snake **skittered** across the sand.
- The **wailing** winds whipped up the sand.
- The desert was dry and **deadly**.

Extension: Describe the following using alliteration:
- the sun's heat
- cold ice.

Task 4

Focus: connectives

- A camel's thick coat protects it from cold **and** keeps out the strong heat from the sun.
- Camels store water in their stomachs **so** they can go days without drinking.
- A camel can live off fat **which** it stores in its hump.

Assessment

RS D can be used for self- and teacher assessment of the work done on the unit challenge spreads.

Extended text

There is an extended text, linked to the unit topic on **RS 10.6**. This can be used in a variety of ways to extend the students' skills and to engage them further.

Great Clarendon Street, Oxford OX2 6DP

Oxford University Press is a department of the University of Oxford.
It furthers the University's objective of excellence in research,
scholarship, and education by publishing worldwide in

Oxford   New York

Auckland   Cape Town   Dar es Salaam   Hong Kong   Karachi
Kuala Lumpur   Madrid   Melbourne   Mexico City   Nairobi
New Delhi   Shanghai   Taipei   Toronto

With offices in

Argentina   Austria   Brazil   Chile   Czech Republic   France   Greece
Guatemala   Hungary   Italy   Japan   Poland   Portugal   Singapore
South Korea   Switzerland   Thailand   Turkey   Ukraine   Vietnam

Oxford is a registered trade mark of Oxford University Press
in the UK and in certain other countries

© Judith Kneen 2006

The moral rights of the author have been asserted

Database right Oxford University Press (maker)

First published 2006

British Library Cataloguing in Publication Data

Data available

ISBN 978-0-19-832555-0

10 9 8 7 6 5

Printed in United Kingdom by Synergie Basingstoke

Acknowledgements
We are grateful for permission to reproduce the following copyright
material:

Interactive activities:

Kit Wright: lines from 'Greedyguts' from *Hot Dog and Other Poems* (Viking
Kestrel, 1981), used by permission of the author.

Resource sheets:

[RS 1.3] 'A Martian Sends a Postcard Home' by Craig Raine from *A Martian
Sends a Postcard Home* (OUP, 1979), copyright © Craig Raine 1979,
reproduced by permission of DGA Ltd for the author.

[RS 1.4] Extract from *Oxford First Encyclopedia* by Andrew Langley (OUP,
2005), copyright © Andrew Langley 1998, reproduced by permission of
Oxford University Press.

[RS 2.3] Headlines, copyright © Guardian Newspapers Ltd 2004,
reproduced by permission of GNL.
1. Alok Jha: 'Out of the blue, a deadly wall of water', *The Guardian*, 27.12.04
2. 'Millions lack food and shelter', *Guardian Unlimited*, 27.12.04
3. Patrick Barkham and Jackie Dent: 'Tourists return after holiday
nightmare', *The Guardian*, 28.12.04
4. Patrick Barkham: 'Boy, two, found by aunt on the Internet', *The Guardian*,
29.12.04
5. Sam Jones: 'One mother's choice...which child to save', *The Guardian*,
31.12.04
6. Mark Tran: 'Please help. Give us aid', *Guardian Unlimited*, 31.12.04
7. Jason Burke: 'Smashed hotel reveals its dead', *The Guardian*, 29.12.04.

[RS 2.4] 'I am the Wind' by Julia Pearson first published in *New English
First* by Rhodri Jones (Heinemann Education, 1988).

[RS 2.6] 'March' by Emily Dickinson from *The Poems of Emily Dickinson*
edited by Thomas H Johnson (The Belknap Press of Harvard University
Press, Cambridge, Massachusetts), copyright © 1951, 1955, 1979, 1983
by the President and Fellows of Harvard College, reproduced by
permission of the publishers and the Trustees of Amherst College.

[RS 3.6] from www.computer.howstuffworks.com

[RS 4.6] Advert for Parachute Jump Experience from
www.thanksdarling.com, reproduced by permission of thanksdarling
Ltd.

[RS 5.6] Extract from *My Story: The Great Plague: The Diary of Alice
Paynton London 1665-1666* by Pamela Oldfield (Scholastic Children's
Books, 2001), text copyright © Pamela Oldfield 2001, reproduced by
permission of Scholastic Ltd. All rights reserved.

[RS 7.6] Extract adapted from www.oxfam.org.uk/coolplanet/teachers
by permission of Oxfam GB, Oxfam House, John Smith Drive, Cowley,
Oxford OX4 2JY, UK. Oxfam GB does not necessarily endorse any text
or activities that acompany the materials nor has it approved the
adapted text.

[RS 8.6] Extract from *The Oxford Children's Book of Famous People* (OUP,
2002), copyright © Oxford University Press 1994, reproduced by
permission of Oxford University Press.

[RS 9.6] Extract from *The Thief of Always* by Clive Barker
(HarperCollins, 1992), copyright © Clive Barker 1992, reproduced by
permission of HarperCollins Publishers Ltd.

[RS 10.6] Desert Survival information from www.phoenix.gov/FIRE,
reproduced by permission of the Phoenix Fire Department, Phoenix,
Arizona, USA.

We have tried to trace and contact all copyright holders before
publication. If notified the publishers will be pleased to rectify any
errors or omissions at the earliest opportunity.

The Publisher would like to thank the following for permission to
reproduce photographs:

Interactive activities:

[Unit 1] Moonwalk: Photodisc/OUP; Saturn: Photodisc/OUP; Space
shuttle landing: NASA; Spiral Galaxy: Photodisc/OUP; Earth from
Space: Photodisc/OUP; Space Walk: Photodisc/OUP; Space shuttle
taking off: Photodisc/OUP; Astronauts: NASA; Comet: Photodisc/OUP;
Life on Mars: NASA.

[Unit 8] Artwork is by Milivoj Ceran/Beehive Illustration.

Resource sheets:

[RS 1.4] Photodisc/Oxford University Press; Unit 4 RS 4.6:
Photodisc/Oxford University Press.

BookMaster Software © e-s-p 2006